JOSEF PIEPER

An Anthology

JOSEF PIEPER

An Anthology

Foreword by
Hans Urs von Balthasar

IGNATIUS PRESS   SAN FRANCISCO

Title of the German original:
Josef Pieper: Lesebuch
© 1981 by Kösel-Verlag GmbH & Co., Munich
Second edition © 1984 by Kösel-Verlag GmbH & Co., Munich

Cover by Victoria Hoke Lane

Contents

The Two Sides of the Coin
That Is Truth

The Freedom of Philosophy
and Its Adversaries

Free Space in
the World of Work

Truths — Known and Believed

The Reality of the Holy

"Finis" Means Both End and Goal

Foreword

In each of his thick little books Josef Pieper is so present to us both as a thinker and a man and reveals himself so openly that it would hardly make sense to write a book *about* him. I was particularly captivated by his wonderful afterword to the German edition of C. S. Lewis' work *The Problem of Pain*, which bears the title "Concerning Plainness of Language in Philosophy". Here he shows that the specialized sciences, which are always abstracting from the meaning of Being as a whole, must develop a precise language and must, indeed, be satisfied with *that*. But the philosopher, who in Goethe's words contemplates the "holy and manifest mystery" of Being and its meaning, does best to keep to that language which always grows out of the wisdom of man as he philosophizes unconsciously. "A word from the treasury of home-grown human language contains more reality than a technical term." And then follows this astounding but accurate statement: "Improbable as this may sound, we can say that not only Lao Tzu, Plato and Augustine but even Aristotle and Thomas Aquinas used no technical terminology." Just these names are a guarantee of the fact that what Pieper means by "plainness" —which for him is "the very seal of credibility"—in no way implies something "flat or even trivial and therefore easy to understand".

Why not? Because the method of each science is the correct one when that science allows itself to be determined and molded by its object. History and psychology are exact in a manner different from the exactness of physics or biology. The following fundamental principle has always remained Pieper's point of departure: to accept the given as it gives

Translated by Erasmo Leiva-Merikakis.

itself, and to allow it its existence as such, in its own truth, goodness and beauty, is the precondition for learning anything about it. And when we come to consider man, it is this same principle that enables us to tell when and how man appears in all the precise truth and excellent strength (*virtus*) proper only to himself. The cardinal virtues as a whole, as interpreted anew by Pieper in the light of Plato and Thomas in his four famous little books, are nothing but man's giving of himself in accordance with his nature as an image of absolute Being.

But how does reality, that "holy and manifest mystery", give itself, and indeed so intensely that Goethe would have us reach out and grasp it "without delay"? Reality always gives itself as something *more* than can be grasped, as an inexhaustible "light that can never be drunk up". As I experience a loving "thou" that gives itself to me, I learn that this "more" —which is the very freedom of the other as he opens himself up to me—cannot be grasped, although at the same time I must also say that it truly does give itself to me and does not withdraw from me.

Pieper's knowledge of the history of philosophy is universal; although he never "shows off", he can when necessary hit the nail on the head with the perfect quotation from a relevant philosophical period, thus clarifying and supporting his meaning. But he is very far from letting things go at half-truths. On occasion he can reply with a sharply resounding "no!" and thus brand himself as one of the Untimely Inopportunes. This he does, for instance, when responding to Descartes' and Bacon's concept of philosophy. Pieper clearly says no to these thinkers' view that philosophy ought to "make us into lords and possessors of nature" and that philosophical theory should be measured by the praxis that produces it. Pieper obviously does not mean that man should not create but that he should create only once he has received. Otherwise man consistently ends up in the atheism that results from his putting himself in the place of the Creator God. This, too, is the reason that Pieper must say no to the supposed high point of modern philosophy, the much-celebrated Hegel, when Hegel makes it his endeavor to have philosophy "approach the goal of shedding its name as 'love of knowledge' in order to become real knowledge": and here "real knowledge" means *absolute knowledge* that causes the mystery of Being to vanish into the dialectical method controlled by reason. And what has become of this demonic reaching for divine knowledge in the case of our contemporary post-Hegelians? Either the empty rattling of word play [*Logistik*], or a hermetic whispering about hermeneutics, or what ultimately becomes the bourgeois subjugation of knowledge under the state (Hegel), under the people (Hitler), or under society and the economy (Marx, Stalin and Americanism).

When we have reached a situation in which nothing "gives" itself any longer or "opens up" to us from within, a situation in which nothing "hands itself over" on its own initiative and in which, therefore, thought is no longer devoted to the deepest interior source of a thing: in such a situation no opening of horizons toward the future remains possible. Only when philosophy is a love-filled longing for the ever-greater mystery of Being, an unconditional longing that propels man down his questing path—only then do we have a reliable basis for that opening up of the future Pieper is always calling for: a reliable basis, in other words, for *hope*.

One final thing also makes Pieper one of the Untimely Inopportunes, that group which as a rule is also the most necessary to a society. If it is true that philosophy is made possible by the fact that Being has manifested itself always *in advance* even if also *in mystery*, then it is also true that philosophy always, and "in advance", has to do with theology. For the Greeks this was something quite evident: for them, philosophy was knowledge searching for the absolute foundation of the world. How is it possible, then, that philosophy in our day has sunk from this height and aligned itself submissively as just another of the specialized sciences, thus demeaning its own nature? Perhaps because Christian theology has likewise set up shop as the (equally specialized) "science" that deals with the manner in which the divine *Urgrund* has revealed itself in Christ. But this turn of events can be dated back only to a rationalist Late Scholasticism and to the influence of Descartes, whereas for the Fathers and High Scholasticism the "awe" of the philosopher before the "holy and manifest mystery" had always been the basis and presupposition for the Christian's love for the God who gives himself wholly in the Old and New Covenants. Here, however, we should not primarily say "love for" but, before all else, "love from". Just as the gracious, faithful and merciful God who made a covenant with Israel requires in the end a reply of perfect love from man, so too Jesus—as our transparency toward God, our very interpreter of God—expects a truly astounding love for himself: "Do you love me more than these?" and "If you love me, keep my commandment." He means the commandment to love, which is the only place where the highest insight into the absolute now opens up. Have the theologians really pondered the question of what "scientific" method is needed by an object who demands the highest of loves for himself? Surely, at the very least, a method that does not seek to master him!

Pieper has always and unashamedly celebrated the inevitable and long-standing marriage feast of philosophy and theology. All his works exist in the only concrete space in our world in which the philosopher cannot help coming to grips positively or negatively with the self-revelation of Being in Jesus Christ. This is the concrete locus where all authentic Christian thinkers of our century have lived: Marcel and Eliot, Lewis and Siewerth, to name only four. Regardless of how much the statement may grate in the ears of modern "specialists", we must affirm that whoever dichotomizes this concrete reality into a philosophy closed in upon itself and a self-contented theology is neither a philosopher nor a theologian.

We owe a great debt of gratitude to Josef Pieper for untiringly saying time and again, in meditations many may find inopportune, those things most necessary for our times.

Hans Urs von Balthasar

Human Authenticity

I

The Ultimate

The last great master of Western Christendom before the schism, Thomas Aquinas, designated human virtue as *ultimum potentiae*, meaning: the utmost best a person can be. It is clear at once that this terse definition does not allow us even to think of associating certain well-known distortions with the word "virtue"; it is not even worthwhile to talk about this matter at length. On the other hand, it would certainly be rewarding to reflect more closely upon some conceptual elements that are contained in this definition but are, at first sight, also somewhat concealed within it.

For example, whenever we speak of the ultimum, of the ultimate and last, we have already thought *implicitly* of a penultimate and first. And with that, something has already been said about the human being: namely, that his everyday life is situated between these different states of realization, disposed toward his ultimate potential but not necessarily reaching it; that the human person is, at the core, someone becoming; in any case, that he is not simply made as this or that, not a purely static entity but an unfolding being, a dynamic reality—just as the cosmos is in its totality. Of course, this is not a distinctly Christian notion. Two thousand years ago, the Greek poet Pindar expressed it in this famous statement: "Become what you are." This says something that seems

Originally published in *Menschliches Richtigsein* (Freiburg im Breisgau: Informationszentrum Berufe der Kirche, 1980). Translated by Margareta Svjagintsev.

truly astonishing, namely, that we are not yet what we already are. Theological wisdom in Christendom is convinced of this, too, when it grants true virtue to that person alone who realizes the utmost of his capacities.

Something specifically Christian, though, reveals itself in the answer to the question of how we ought to imagine the very earliest beginning of this event of self-realization. Obviously, the beginning is given. It is not as if a human being, once he freely does good, were setting his foot for the first time upon a path not trodden before or even prepared. Rather, all ethical action, meaning all human action based upon decision and responsibility, is only a continuation and expansion of something begun long ago and still in progress. "It" wills to reach the goal fittingly set for man long before he makes free decisions; like an arrow shot, it flies on its way. Christian theology speaks here of a "nature-given" will, of an *impetus* innately given "by nature" that we "obey" when we do good. But these statements about human "nature" and its "nature-given" will are only, so to speak, something tentative and provisional. We only comprehend them properly when we understand by human "nature" the sum total of what is suggested by virtue of having been created human. By the act of creating him, God sets the human being upon the path whose goal is that "ultimate" which can be called "virtue" in its true sense: the realization of the divine design incorporated in the creature.

Reflecting upon this, we may have an inkling of the almost unreachable challenge conveyed by the notion of "virtue". And perhaps suddenly the pointed New Testament expression may be less enigmatic: "No one is good—but God alone" (Mk 10:18).

2

A Dead Word?

A few years ago, a speech on virtue was given before the French Academy by Paul Valéry. In this speech he said: "Virtue, ladies and gentlemen, the word virtue is dead." This is how we've ended up, with the word "virtue" "now found only in catechisms, in jokes, in the universities and in operettas". The diagnosis is doubtless true, but one should not be too surprised about it. We are dealing here in part with a completely natural phenomenon, the natural fate of "great words". And then: Why, in a dechristianized world, should we doubt the effectiveness of demonic developments of speech by which the "customary use of words" for the good is made ridiculous? Finally and above all, apart from those above-mentioned possibilities that need to be taken seriously, we must not forget that Christian moral literature and moral proclamation did not always make it easy for the common man to recognize the authentic meaning of the concept and reality of "virtue".

Virtue does not mean being "nice" and "proper" in an isolated act or omission. Virtue means: man's being "is" right, and this in the supernatural and natural sense. Here we find two dangerous possibilities for perverting the notion of virtue within the Christian common consciousness itself: first, there is the possibility of moralism, which isolates the action, the

Originally published in *Über das christliche Menschenbild* (Leipzig: Hegner Verlag, 1964). Translated by Margareta Svjagintsev.

"performance", the "exercise" and makes it independent from the living existence of a vital human being; and second, there is the possibility of supernaturalism, which diminishes the value of the natural well-lived life, of vitality and of natural decency and integrity. Virtue is also, very generally, an essential enhancement of the human person; it is the fulfillment of human potential—in the natural as well as in the supernatural domain. This is how the virtuous man "is": by the innermost tendency of his being he realizes the good by doing it.

3

"Ought To"

First and foremost, a presupposition must be clarified and then accepted, namely, the belief that a man "ought to", in other words, that not everything in his action and behavior is well and good just as it is. It makes no sense trying to convince a pig it ought to act and behave "like a real pig". That the rude line by Gottfried Benn—"The crown of creation: the pig, man"—can be spoken at all and, further, hold true in such terrible ways: this fact alone shows that humanity must still realize the truly human in the domain of lived realities; it means man, as long as he exists, "ought to". Of course, one can formulate the concept somewhat less aggressively than Gottfried

Originally published in "Die Aktualität der Kardinaltugenden", *Buchstabier-Übungen* (Munich: Kösel-Verlag, 1980). Translated by Margareta Svjagintsev.

Benn. In this way, for example: "Fire does by necessity what is true and right according to its being, not so man, when he is doing the good." This is a sentence from Anselm of Canterbury's *Dialogue on Truth*. Two statements are thereby made: man (on the one hand) is free; and (on the other hand) meaning is given to him regardless of his opinion or his permission. It is precisely this last fact that all existentialism resists and, as it reaches far beyond the domain of a special philosophical school, also determines the common attitude of the people of our time; this is exactly what Jean-Paul Sartre's famous sentence means: "There is no such thing as human nature!" To one who does not acknowledge that the human being "is" homo sapiens in a totally different manner than water "is" H_2O; that, to the contrary, the human being must *become* what he is and therefore not already (*eo ipso* "is"); that one can speak of all other earthly creatures in the indicative, in simple statements, but of man, if one wants to hit upon his actual reality, one can only speak in the imperative —to him who cannot see this or does not want to admit to its truth it would be understandably meaningless to speak at all of an "ought to" and it would make no sense to give instructions on obligation, be it in the form of a teaching on virtue or otherwise.

4

Seven Statements

The wisdom of the West expresses the sum total of what man "ought to" do in seven sentences:

First: Man, insofar as he realizes his meaning, is someone who—in *faith*—opens himself by listening to God's word, whenever he can perceive it.

Second: Man is true to himself only when he is stretching forth—in *hope*—toward a fulfillment that cannot be reached in his bodily existence.

Third: The man who strives for fulfillment is someone who—in *love* (*caritas*)—partakes in the eternally affirmative power of the Creator himself and, with all the strength of his being, finds it good that God, the world and he himself exist.

Fourth: Man's life is authentic only when he does not allow his vision of reality to be clouded by the yes or no of his own desire; on the contrary, his decisionmaking and action depend upon reality revealing itself to him. By his willingness to live the truth he shows himself to be *prudent*.

Fifth: The good man is above all *just*, which means he understands how to be a companion. He possesses the art of living with others in such a way that he gives to each what is rightfully his.

Sixth: The man who is prudent and just knows that it is necessary to put himself on the line in order to realize the good

---

Unpublished lecture, manuscript. Translated by Margareta Svjagintsev.

in this world. He is ready—with *courage*—to accept loss and injuries for the sake of truth and justice.

Seventh: To the authenticity of man belongs the virtue of *temperance* or *self-discipline* that protects him from the self-destruction of pleasure seeking.

5

Three Streams of Life

The supernatural life in man has three main currents: the reality of God, which surpasses all natural knowledge "not only of men, but also of angels", manifests itself to faith. Love affirms—also in its own right—the Highest Good, which has become visible beneath the veil of faith. Hope is the confidently patient expectation of eternal beatitude in a contemplative and comprehensive sharing of the triune life of God; hope expects from God's hand the eternal life that is God himself: *sperat Deum a Deo*.

The existential relationship of these three—faith, hope, love—can be expressed in three sentences. First: faith, hope and love have all three been implanted in human nature as natural inclinations (*habitus*) conjointly with the reality of grace, the one source of all supernatural life. Second: in the orderly sequence of the active development of these supernatural inclinations, faith takes precedence over both hope and love;

On Hope, pp. 30–31, translated by Sister Mary Francis McCarthy, S.N.D. © 1986 by Ignatius Press, San Francisco. Originally published as *Über die Hoffnung* by Kösel-Verlag, seventh edition © 1977.

hope takes precedence over love; conversely, in the culpable disorder of their dissolution, love is lost first, then hope, and, last of all, faith. Third: in the order of perfection, love holds first place, with faith last, and hope between them.

6

"This Is How It Is"

When someone asks me: "Do you believe this?", what more does he actually desire to know about me? Someone gives me some news to read or he reads it to me, some report that he himself seems to consider astonishing, even incredible; and then he looks me in the eye and asks: "Do you believe that?" Obviously he wants to know whether I accept the account as correct, as true, and its content as an actual event, as reality.

Looking at it from a purely abstract point of view, I might have several possibilities for an answer, not merely "yes", not merely "no". I could shrug my shoulders and say: "I don't know, it may be correct; but perhaps it may just as well not be." I also might possibly say this: "Well, I tend to think there may be something to it, though I am, of course, not absolutely sure it could not be otherwise." Perhaps I could say with total certainty: "No, I don't accept the report as true." This would mean, to formulate it positively: "I take the communication to be false, to be an error, perhaps a lie."

Was heisst Glauben?, originally published in *Vierundzwanzig-Rundfunk-Ansprachen* (Köln: Adamas-Verlag, 1966). Translated by Margareta Svjagintsev.

My "no" could certainly also mean something very different, namely, the following: "You ask me whether I believe
what is said here. This will make you laugh, but I don't believe it and yet I say the report is true! Well, as fate would have
it, I saw the reported event myself with my own eyes. I do not
believe it to be true, I *know* it is." And finally, of course, there
is yet another possibility, which I say after a little while: "Yes,
I believe it happened exactly as it is written here." This,
though, I would perhaps say only after I had ascertained the
identity of the reporter or the newspaper in which the information is printed.

In any case, we have inadvertently demonstrated here the
four classic basic forms of comment on a state of affairs:
doubting, supposing, knowing and believing. We disregard
disbelief (taking the report to be a lie) at this point because it
is basically a positive viewpoint that in turn can reassume the
form of supposing or knowing or believing.

The one who knows and the one who believes have one
thing in common. They both state: "Yes, it is so, and not otherwise." They both unhesitatingly accept the matter reported
as true.

There is one point—a very important one, to be sure—at
which knowledge and faith, the knower and the believer, are
distinctly different: when the one who knows has insight into
the facts being discussed; the believer, in contrast, can *not*
know the actual event by his own experience. How can he
then say: "It is so and not otherwise"?

Herein lies the whole problem of "faith", not just the concept but also the practice: the theoretical difficulty of conceiv-
ing of the dynamics of faith and the practical difficulty of being able to make faith a living act, to be responsible for it and
to justify it.

To the question of how the believing person can say: "It is
so and not otherwise", my answer is: "He can say it because
he puts his trust in another who guarantees the facts." Unlike
the knower, the believer is not only involved with factual

circumstances but also and above all with someone, with the person of the witness in whom the believer puts his trust.

7

Sharing in Knowledge

To believe means: to participate in the knowledge of a knower. If, therefore, there is no one who sees and knows, then, properly speaking, there can be no one who believes. A fact which everyone knows because it is obvious can no more be the subject of belief than a fact which no one knows—and whose existence, therefore, no one can vouch for. Belief cannot establish its own legitimacy; it can only derive legitimacy from someone who knows the subject matter of his own accord. By virtue of contact with this someone, belief is transmitted to the believer.

There are several statements implicit in this proposition. To begin with: belief is by its nature something *secondary*. Wherever belief is meaningfully held, there is someone else who supports the believer; and this someone else cannot be a believer. Before belief, therefore, come seeing and knowing. These take precedence over belief. Any serious examination of human modes of thinking and speaking will bear this out. The same obtains for the concept of belief in Western theology. Neither the theological nor the epistemological approach will

Belief and Faith, pp. 32–42, translated by Richard and Clara Winston. © 1963 by Random House, Inc., New York. Reprinted with permission of Pantheon Books, Inc., New York.

permit us to elevate belief into something supreme and sub-lime which cannot be surpassed. Thus, Newman states rather sternly: "Faith, then, must necessarily be resolvable at last into Sight and Reason; unless, indeed, we agree with enthusiasts."

Therefore, when we rank belief as secondary to seeing and knowing, we are not going counter to the traditional doctrine of belief. Rather, we are completely in accord with that doctrine. *Visio est certior auditu*, says Thomas; seeing is surer than hearing. That is to say, in seeing for ourselves we are achiev-ing more contact with reality and are in greater possession of reality than when we espouse knowledge based upon hearing.

This statement, to be sure, promptly calls for an important addition or, we might also say, a correction. The aphorism quoted from the *Summa theologica* was quoted only partially. The entire statement is as follows: *ceteris paribus visio est certior auditu*; that is, *under otherwise similar conditions* seeing is surer than hearing. That is to say: if both possibilities are equally available to us, if we have the choice — then we choose knowl-edge based on seeing, and not knowledge based on hearing.

But perhaps man's situation is that he cannot choose, or at any rate, not always. What is he to do when decision lies be-tween *either* no access whatsoever to a given subject matter *or* knowledge on the basis of hearing; *either* incomplete knowing *or* no knowing at all? The fact remains, as we have said, that *ceteris paribus* seeing for oneself is surer than hearing. But what if seeing for oneself is impossible? Should we then, instead of accepting a less than complete access to reality as the best we can hope for, rather forgo all access, following the heroic maxim: "All or nothing"? That precisely is the question each man confronts when he has to decide between belief and non-belief.

Let us take the case of a naturalist who around the year 1700 has set himself the task of describing the pollen grains of the flowers he knows. No doubt he would be able, with the naked eye and the aid of simple magnifying glasses, to find out a good deal by "seeing for himself". But suppose he is visited by a colleague who has seen such pollen at Delft under one of the first microscopes made by Anton van Leeuwenhoek. Suppose this visitor tells him that the black dust which adheres to one's hand when one brushes a poppy is in fact a mass of geometric structures of extremely regular shapes which can be clearly differentiated from the pollen granules of all other flowering plants — and so on. Let us assume further that our naturalist has had no opportunity to look through a microscope himself, and has never observed these things which his visitor reports. Granted these assumptions, would not our naturalist be grasping more truth, which means more reality, if he did *not* insist on regarding as true and real only what he has seen with his own eyes, if on the contrary he could bring himself to "believe" his visitor? In such a situation, what about the ranking of knowledge based upon seeing for oneself and knowledge based upon hearing? Does not hearing and believing take precedence?

Here is the point for us to present in its entirety the sentence of Thomas which we have hitherto abbreviated: "Under otherwise similar conditions seeing is surer than hearing; but if the one from whom we learn something by hearing is capable of grasping far more than one could obtain by seeing for oneself, then hearing is surer than seeing." Naturally this sentence was originally formulated in regard to belief in the theological sense. But it is equally true of all kinds of belief; belief has the extraordinary property of endowing the believer with knowledge which would not be available to him by the exercise of his own powers.

A dictum from Hesiod's *Works and Days* makes the very same point. As Hesiod puts it, being wise with the head of someone else is undoubtedly a smaller thing than possessing knowledge oneself, but it is far to be preferred to the sterile arrogance of one who does not achieve the independence of the knower and simultaneously despises the dependence of the believer.

Before we, as believers, accept the testimony of another, we must be sure that he has authentic knowledge of those things which we accept on faith. If he himself is, in his turn, only a believer, then we are misplacing our reliance. It becomes clear, therefore, that this reliance itself, which is the decisive factor in the act of belief, must be founded upon some knowledge on the part of the believer if it is to be valid. This is still another aspect of the proposition that belief rests upon knowledge.

To be sure, trusting reliance is by nature a free act. No argumentation, no matter how "compelling", can actually bring us to "believe" in someone else. Nevertheless this act does not take place in a vacuum and without reason—without, for example, some conviction of the credibility of the witness on whom we rely. But this conviction in turn cannot possibly be belief; the credibility of the witness whom we believe cannot also be the subject of belief; this is where real knowledge is required. The matter is, to be sure, somewhat complicated.

Let us return to our example of the returned prisoner of war. We can single out fairly clearly the element which requires belief. It is the information that my brother is alive. Let us say I have assured myself of the reliability and credibility of the witness by checking up, by sharp observation and direct experience. On the other hand, the credibility of the man might be underwritten for me by someone else, by one of my friends, say, who I discover knows my informant very well. In such a situation it would once again be an act of belief which assured me of my visitor's credibility. Nevertheless, it is clear that the conviction, "My brother is alive", not only has a different content and has come about in a different way from the conviction, "My informant is trustworthy", but also that these two acts of belief are based upon two altogether different testimonies from two different witnesses. In short, we see that the premises of belief cannot be the object of that same belief.

The real implications of this thesis dramatically come to light in the theological realm. We might imagine the following dialogue: "On the basis of what, really, are you convinced that there is an Eternal Life?" — "On the basis of divine Revelation; he who is the absolute Knower and the absolute Truth has said so, and I *believe* him." — "On the basis of what are you so sure that anything like God exists and that he is absolutely knowing and truthful?" We obviously cannot simply respond: "I believe it." To put the matter more cautiously, there must at least be a possibility of responding: "I know it."

But the following question might also be asked in that dialogue: "On the basis of what are you certain that God has spoken at all and that he has actually said there is Eternal Life?"

Here, again, we could not legitimately respond with a simple profession of belief.

If man is prohibited from obtaining by his natural powers some kind of knowledge that God exists, that he is Truth itself, that he actually has spoken to us, and that this divine speech has said and meant thus and so — then belief in revelation is likewise not possible as a meaningful human act. (By a *human* act theology also understands the act of "supernatural", "infused" faith, for we ourselves are the ones who do the believing!) To put this as sharply as possible: if *everything* is said to be belief, then belief has been eliminated.

This very thing underlies the old idea of the *praeambula fidei*; the premises of belief are not a part of what the believer believes. They pertain rather to that which he knows, or at least must be able to know. It is another matter that in the ordinary course of events only a few really know what is in itself knowable. In any case this does not detract from the validity of the proposition: *cognitio fidei praesupponit cognitionem naturalem*. Belief does not presuppose knowledge based upon belief in its turn dependent upon someone else, but rather knowledge out of one's own resources.

Nowhere, to be sure, will we find it written that this *cognitio naturalis* must always or primarily be derived by means of rational deduction. "Credibility", for example, is a quality of persons, and can only be known in the same manner as we apprehend the other personal qualities of a person. In this realm, of course, syllogistic argumentation plays only the most minor part. When we direct our gaze upon a human being, we engage in a rapid, penetrating and direct cognition of a unique kind. Certainly we bring nothing of the sort to our examination of facts of nature, however earnest and searching this may be. On the other hand, such "intuitive" knowledge may be neither verifiable nor provable. Socrates declared that he could recognize a lover at once. *By what signs* do we recognize things of that sort? No one, not even Socrates, has ever been able to answer this question in a way that can be checked and demonstrated. Yet Socrates would stoutly insist that this knowledge was no mere impression, but objective, true knowledge, that is to say, knowledge which had risen out of contact with reality.

Of course we do not intend in the least to deny the necessity and the importance of rationally demonstrative argumentation (for the existence of God, say, or for the historical authenticity of the Bible), especially in the realm of religious truth. But it is equally evident to me that we might say: Whoever undertakes to defend belief against the arguments of rationalism should prepare himself by considering the question: "How do we apprehend a person?"

8

Communication of Reality

According to the theologians, the essence of the Christian faith can be summed up in two words. Those two words are Trinity and Incarnation. The "universal teacher" of Christendom has said that the whole content of the truth of Christian faith can be reduced to the dogma of the Trinitarian God and the dogma that man participates in the life of God through Christ.

(The outsider, who has the impression of a bewildering multiplicity of dogmas and ideas, will ask himself: What about all the rest; what about the knotty problems of sacraments and sacramentals, hell and "purgatory", veneration of Mary, cult of saints, visions, "apparitions", and so on? As regards the last two items—which in fact can occasionally obscure a view of the essentials—it should be clearly understood that they fall outside the category of things which we are required to accept on the testimony of God. Even the Church's "acknowledgement" of certain apparitions means no more than the following: first, that nothing about these phenomena offends against the Faith or the ethical principles of life; and secondly, that there are sufficient signs attesting that these things may be considered true and genuine *fide humana*, on *human* testimony; for which reason, thirdly, it is not right simply to despise them. But all the rest—the dogma of the sacraments, of the

Belief and Faith, pp. 88–91, translated by Richard and Clara Winston. © 1963 by Random House, Inc., New York. Reprinted with permission of Pantheon Books, Inc., New York.

Blessed Virgin, of the Last Things—can really be reduced to the two tenets named by Thomas Aquinas. This matter, however, can be conveyed only to one who already believes.)

Such is the character of this basically unitary content of divine revelation that the reality it affirms is, in a peculiar fashion, identical with the act of revelation and also with the witness. This is a situation almost without parallel anywhere else in the world. The "almost" is intended to leave room for the possibly sole exception, for the situation in which a person turns to another and says: "I love you." That statement, too, is not primarily supposed to inform another person of an objective fact separable from the speaker. Rather, it is a kind of self-witnessing; and the witnessed subject matter is given reality solely by having been spoken in such a manner. In keeping with this condition, the only way the partner can become aware of the love that is offered is by taking what is said into himself, by listening. Of course, the state of being loved can simply happen to him, as to an immature child; but he can truly "know" it only by hearing the verbal avowal and "believing" it only then will the other's love become truly present to him; only then will he truly partake of it.

On a higher plane, the very same rule applies to divine revelation. In speaking to men God does not cause them to know objective facts, but he does throw open to them his own Being. The subject matter which forms the essential content of revelation—that man has been elected to participate in the divine life; that that divine life has been offered to him, in fact already given—this subject matter owes its reality to nothing but the fact that it is pronounced by God. It is real in that God reveals it. The situation is not that the "Incarnation" exists "anyhow" as a fact and is subsequently made known by the revelation. Rather, the Incarnation of God and the revelation in Christ are one and the same reality. For the believer there is once more the experience that he, in accepting the message of the self-revealing God, actually partakes of the divine life therein announced. There is no other way in which he could partake of it, save by belief. It is imparted to him—here the word "impart" is restored to its original meaning. Divine revelation is not an announcement of a report on reality, but the "imparting" of reality itself. That imparting takes effect, however, only upon the believer.

9

To Hope—But on What Grounds?

Everyone knows that "success" in life, carrying through our existence as a whole to a good end, has been termed "salvation" since time immemorial. It is that complete well-being toward which "true" hope is pointing. But what does that salvation consist of? This question, to be clear from the beginning, can be meaningfully considered only if one is ready to bring the above viewpoints into play. He who wants to avoid this task has already denied himself the opportunity to speak seriously on the subject of human hope.

The great teachers of the Christian West designated hope unmistakably as a "theological virtue". There is something deeply disquieting in this that cannot easily be resolved. For this is what is stated: it does not in the least challenge the right for hope within history, not at all; still, the human being is not

"Hoffnung—auf was?", originally published in *Tradition als Herausforderung* (Munich: Kösel-Verlag, 1963). Translated by Margareta Svjagintsev.

automatically well ordered just because he sets his hope on natural well-being, even though it may be something as great as peace on earth and just order among nations. It is said that only the hope for God-given salvation, for eternal life, sets man right from within. (This is what is meant by the concept of "virtue": to be set right.) One needs to be aware of the inner tension of this thesis. Not only does it renounce an activism totally enclosed within the plane of history and insistent that no hope is left when there is nothing more we can do; it also renounces the mere otherworldliness of a supernaturalism excluding history, which would abandon political humanity to fatalism. The disquiet set in motion by the thesis of the "theological" character of hope is decisive even in the present opposition of Marxism-Christianity. But the most disquieting fact is the decisiveness of realizing the insight Plato had already glimpsed: the "greatest hope" can be fulfilled only on condition of being initiated into the mysteries.

In this connection the answer to another important question can be found: not "hope—for what?", but "hope—on what grounds?" The holy book of Christian faith has given the answer in this way: the virtue hope is nothing "if Christ has not risen".

The Obscurity of Hope and Despair

There is a despair that is not easily recognizable as despair. And there is a hope that, to the superficial glance, may seem to be nothing but despair, even though it is hope of a most triumphant kind. Precisely this I call the "obscurity" of hope as well as of despair. I am not saying that every hope and all despair are necessarily always hard to identify; I only say, it is possible that hope as well as despair may appear at first sight in an unrecognizable form. We shall discuss this in the following.

Soren Kierkegaard gave to the obscure kind of despair the name "despair of weakness". This despair, he says, consists of man not daring to be himself, even explicitly not wanting to be himself. He refuses to be what he truly is, he does not accept his own essence.

By this concept, "despair of weakness", Kierkegaard returned, consciously or unconsciously, to an ancient thought of Western wisdom, namely, the notion of that special kind of "sloth" that, as *acedia*, is habitually counted among the seven capital sins (*vitia capitalia*). But present-day popular understanding has perverted the original concept of "sloth" as a capital sin into nearly its opposite. In ordinary usage "sloth" seems to have settled into the domain of work—understood as lack of diligence, laziness, lack of pleasure in work. But when

---

"Die Verborgenheit von Hoffnung and Verzweiflung", originally published in *Tradition als Herausforderung* (Munich: Kösel-Verlag, 1963). Translated by Margareta Svjagintsev.

the great masters of Western Christendom named this "sloth of the heart" a sin, it was not meant to be an approval of the ceaseless activity of the capitalist work establishment. Rather, *acedia* means that man does not "col-laborate" or work together with the realization of himself; that he refuses to add his conscious contribution to his very own, truly human existence. It is not at all a question of external activity but of the full realization of the self, to which we know we are silently but unmistakably summoned. And *not* to accept this summons, to respond to it with "no": this is precisely the essence of "sloth", of *acedia*. Through the sloth that is sin, man barricades himself against the challenge handed to him by his own dignity. He resists being a spiritual entity endowed with the power to make decisions; he simply does not want to be that for which God lifted him up above all natural potentiality. In other words, man does not want to be what he nevertheless cannot stop being: a spiritual being, truly satisfied with nothing less than God himself; and beyond that, "son of God", rightful heir to eternal life.

The ancients, too, thought of sloth and despair as belonging together. They call *acedia* a form of sadness, namely, that paralyzing *tristitia saeculi* of which Paul says that it brings death. But not only that. The ancients say explicitly that this sadness is already the beginning of despair—just as Kierkegaard understands the "despair of weakness" as the first step to actual and complete despair, the reflected "despair of self-assertion". But where is that "obscurity" and "deception" which must be unmasked and exposed with special care?

It was already said that sloth, *acedia*, was considered a capital sin in the ancient wisdom. *Caput* means source. *Vitia capitalia* are those perversions from which, as from a fountainhead, more perversions gush forth. Thus it is meaningful and necessary to speak not only of the source itself, but of the whole length of the river nourished by it. If one proceeds in this manner, from the river's mouth to its source, to the source-sin of sloth, then its relationship to the existential mode of man in our time suddenly becomes very apparent. It is totally impossible to overlook.

From not-wanting-to-be-oneself, from the refusal to collaborate with the completion of one's own being, from this innermost conflict of man with himself, from this sloth (in a word), as the ancients say, springs the "roaming restlessness of the spirit". He who is in conflict with himself in his inmost dwelling, who consequently does not will to be what he fundamentally is anyway, cannot dwell within himself and cannot be at home with himself. He has to make the vain experiment of breaking out from his own center—for example, into the restlessness of working for work's sake or into the insatiable curiosity of the lustful eye, which does not really seek knowledge but only an "opportunity to abandon oneself to the world" (Heidegger), which is an opportunity to avoid oneself.

It must further be realized that both manifestations—the systematic establishment of the work ideal as absolute and the degeneration of the lustful eye—surround themselves with the immense effort of a forced optimism, of a radiating trust in life, of a noisily proclaimed "progress". Everyone knows that belief in progress is declared a social duty in the world of nothing but work. It is also known that *keep happy* and *happy end* belong from the start to the basic elements of this world of illusions, in which the greedy eye has created for itself a replacement for the "fullness of life".

For all that, these optimistic attitudes provide no final meaning in the face of the despair that is their source—even though this source is safely enclosed in the innermost chamber of the heart, so that no cry of pain penetrates to the outside, most likely not even to its own consciousness.

But there is also an obscure form of hope. We still need to speak of it.

All hope says: it will be good, it will end well—with all creation, with man, also with me. The Christian's hope, too, means nothing else. The "good end" here is called: eternal life, salvation, beatitude, new heaven and new earth.

The Christian's hope, however, cannot be separated from certain concepts about the structure of the world of history. And this is the reason that this hope, in the extreme case, can take on so much of the nature of obscurity that to the eye of the non-Christian it is nearly unrecognizable and comes to be seen almost as despair. This idea of the world of history, the world of humanity, says above all that evil possesses power in this world, going even so far as to say that evil, seen from a standpoint inside the world, may appear to be the superior power. The virtue of courage, for example, was always understood to be in itself, as Augustine says, an irrefutable sign of the existence and power of evil in the world. This explains what is in fact not so obvious, that in the Christian understanding of existence the highest incarnation of courage is not the powerful hero in arms but the martyr and that the highest act of courage is the testimony of blood.

For the martyr, to speak in worldly terms, there is no hope left; he is abandoned helplessly to the superior power of evil. Every vital optimism then becomes meaningless, and the natural ability to battle is literally handcuffed. For all that, the phenomenon of the martyr is unthinkable without a sheer triumphal strength of hope. This is the very hope of which I said it is so obscure as to be almost unrecognizable — not simply for the world and the non-Christian, but for the average Christian himself.

In the very obscurity of the martyr's hope a main feature of all true Christian hope is visible: namely, that hope is a *theological virtue*. There is also a natural hope, obviously. But this natural hope is not a virtue because it is hope; this fact alone would not make it part of the true inner order of man. To put it more concretely: man is not set in the "true inner order" simply because he hopes for a happy old age or for the well-being of his children or for peace on earth or even that humanity may be saved from destroying itself. There can be no objection to any of these hopes; and one can call anyone blessed who is able to devote himself to them with undoubting confidence. But who would want to say that such hope belongs to the condition of being set right inwardly, simply meaning it to be a human "virtue"? This is a very different matter in the case of justice! The justice of natural man is also virtue. Hope only becomes virtue as *theological* hope, however, meaning a hope moving toward salvation, which does not exist in the natural world.

Even so, Christian hope does not fail to keep our historical created world in sight as well. One can read this, too, from the character of the Christian martyr. The Christian martyr is something truly incomparable. It is not enough to look at him as a man who dies for his conviction—as if the truth of this conviction did not matter. The distinction and the uniqueness of the Christian witness lies in the fact that in spite of the terror befalling him, from his mouth "no word against God's creation is heard" (E. Peterson).

In the martyr's hope three elements are joined together. The one thing truly hoped for is eternal life and not happiness found in the world. This is the first element. The second is the active "yes" to the created world in all its realms. The third element is the acceptance of a catastrophic end to the world of history.

The connection of these three elements is, logically, filled with dynamic tension; it is not easy to hold these tensions together and endure them. It means that the Christian's hope is naturally always tempted to yield to an impermissible simplification—to a supernaturalism excluding history or to a pure activism within history or to a tragic attitude that is fatalistic and hostile to creation. And indeed, a detached examination of facts will come across such perversions of Christian hope again and again. Obviously, these perversions are not really founded on a difficulty in theoretical knowledge. It is primarily not man as he thinks but man as he spiritually exists in direct experience who is challenged when he is obliged to accept the apocalyptic dimension of history.

It therefore makes little sense to want to interpret and justify the painful silence of the martyr by means of rational argument: in this manner his hope does not emerge from its obscurity. Better and other ways are needed, it seems, than mere reflection and mental effort, if we are to succeed in perceiving the reality of that which lies in obscurity—the reality of the worldly man's hidden despair as well as the victorious reality of the martyr's hidden hope.

I I

Creative Affirmation

If according to the many voices of language love is both something that we "practice" and do as conscious actors, and also something that comes over us and happens to us like an enchantment; if on the one hand it is an emotion directed toward possessing and enjoying, and on the other hand a gesture of self-forgetful surrender and giving which precisely "does not seek its own advantage"; if it is a turning toward someone, possibly God, or other human beings (a friend, a sweetheart, a son, an unknown who needs our help), but possibly also toward the manifold good things of life (sports, science, wine, song); if, finally, it is an act that is ascribed to God himself and even in a certain sense is said to be identical with him ("God is love")—if all this is so, does it not seem rather improbable that any kind of common element can be assumed to lie behind all these phenomena? In other words, is there any

About Love, pp. 18–20, 26–28, translated by Richard and Clara Winston. © 1974 by Franciscan Herald Press, Chicago. Reprinted with permission.

meaning at all to the universal question: What is the "nature" of love? On the other hand, we are inclined to feel from the start that the fact of there being one single word for all this cannot be entirely without some foundation in reality. But if the recurrent identity underlying the countless forms of love does exist, how can it be more exactly described?

My tentative answer to this question runs as follows: In every conceivable case love signifies much the same as approval. This is first of all to be taken in the literal sense of the word's root: loving someone or something means finding him or it *probus*, the Latin word for "good". It is a way of turning to him or it and saying, "It's good that you exist; it's good that you are in this world!"

To avert possible misunderstandings we must elaborate, and almost correct, this definition. I do not mean that the act of love necessarily involves any such bare statement, although that is quite possible. The approval I am speaking of is rather an expression of the *will*. It signifies the opposite of aloof, purely "theoretical" neutrality. It testifies to being in agreement, assenting, consenting, applauding, affirming, praising, glorifying and hailing. Distinct as the difference in intensity is between mere agreement and enthusiastic affirmation, there is one common element in all the members of this series — which, of course, could easily be extended. All the members are without exceptions forms of expression of the will. All of them mean: I want you (or it) to exist! Loving is therefore a mode of willing. If we are somewhat taken aback at this point, to put it mildly, that is due to the narrow conception of willing impressed upon us by certain philosophical and psychological doctrines. We have been taught to restrict the concept of willing to the idea of willing *to do*, in compliance with a much-quoted definition stating that "real willing" means "deciding in favor of actions on the basis of motives". Such activistic restriction has, quite characteristically, also been applied to the concept of knowing — as though knowing consisted solely in the "rational work" of logical thinking and not just as much in the form of "simple intuition" in which we are immediately certain of precisely the fundamental subjects of thinking, such as existence. Thinking is "discursive"—still on the "course" to its own proper result; it is, we might put it, knowledge of what is absent. But what the thinking mind is still seeking the intuiting mind has already found; it is present to it and before its gaze; its eye "rests" upon it. Seeing, intuiting, in contrast to thinking has, it has been said, no "tension towards the future".

Precisely in the same way there is a form of willing which does not aim at doing something still undone, and thus acting in the future to change the present state of affairs. Rather, in addition to willing-to-do there is also a purely affirmative assent to what already is, and this assent is likewise without "future tension"; *le consentement est sans futur*. To confirm and affirm something already accomplished—that is precisely what is meant by "to love". It is true that the will, as Thomas Aquinas once remarks, is usually called a "striving force", *vis appetitiva*. "But the will knows not only the act of striving for what it does not yet have, but also the other act: of loving what it already possesses, and rejoicing in that." A French commentator on Thomas actually distinguishes, in keeping with this pronouncement, between the will as a "force of love" (*puissance d'amour*) and the will as a force for deciding upon choices. . . .

But then, if a human being already exists anyhow, could we not say that it does not matter whether a lover finds it wonderful and affirms it? Does it really add or take away anything that someone says, "It's good that you exist"?

It is clear that in asking this question, which sounds so extremely "realistic", we are basically asking what is the "function" of love within the whole of existence; what it is supposed to do and accomplish in the world. It is one and the same question that we have to answer at this point. But in

order to answer this it admittedly does not suffice to analyze,
no matter how precisely, the lover's intention and what is
"really" willed and meant by the one who feels loving concern. We must move across to the other shore, that is, we
must examine the matter from the point of view of the person
who happens to be loved. What is really taking place on his
side? Soberly considered, what does it mean for a person that
another turns to him and says (or thinks, or experiences), "It's
good that you exist"?

On this matter let me first give the floor to Jean-Paul Sartre,
a writer from whom we should have expected a radically different answer from the one he actually gives. According to the
"theory" he has systematically developed, every human being
is in principle alien to every other, who by looking at him
threatens to steal the world from him; everyone is a danger to
everyone else's existence, a potential executioner. But fortu-
nately, the creative artist in Sartre, or simply the brilliant observer and describer of human reality, repeatedly rises up
against merely intellectual theses. And the artist in him, altogether unconcerned about his own "philosophy", will then
say things like this: "This is the basis for the joy of love . . .:
we feel that our existence is justified." As may be seen, that is
not so very far from the above-mentioned notions of "giving
existence" and "conferring the right to exist". Here, however, the matter is seen not from the lover's point of view, but
from that of the beloved. Obviously, then, it does not suffice
us simply to exist; we can do that "anyhow". What matters to
us, beyond mere existence, is the explicit confirmation: It is
good that you exist; how wonderful that you are! In other
words, what we need over and above sheer existence is: to be
loved by another person. That is an astonishing fact when we
consider it closely. Being created by God actually does not
suffice, it would seem; the fact of creation needs continuation
and perfection by the creative power of human love.

But this seemingly astonishing fact is repeatedly confirmed
by the most palpable experience, of the kind that everyone has

day after day. We say that a person "blossoms" when undergoing the experience of being loved; that he becomes wholly himself for the first time; that a "new life" is beginning for him—and so forth. For a child, and to all appearances even for the still unborn child, being loved by the mother is literally *the* precondition for its own thriving. This material love need not necessarily be "materialized" in specific acts of beneficence. What is at any rate more decisive is that concern and approval which are given from the very core of existence—we need not hesitate to say, which come from the heart—and which are directed toward the core of existence, the heart, of the child. Only such concern and approval do we call real "love". The observations of René Spitz have become fairly well known. He studied children born in prison and brought up in scarcely comfortable outward conditions by their imprisoned mother. These he compared with other children raised without their mothers, but in well-equipped, hygienically impeccable American infants' and children's homes by excellently trained nurses. The result of the comparison is scarcely surprising: in regard to illness, mortality and susceptibility to neuroses, the children raised in prison were far better off. Not that the nurses had performed their tasks in a merely routine matter and with "cold objectivity". But it is simply not enough to be able to eat to satiation, not to freeze, to have a roof overhead and everything else that is essential to life. The institutionalized children had all such needs satisfied. They received plenty of "milk"; what was lacking was—the "honey". This allusion to the biblical metaphor of the "land flowing with milk and honey" (Ex 3:8) is to be found in the masterly essay by Erich Fromm, *The Art of Loving*, which has had unusual success as a book. (That success may have had something to do with a misunderstanding assiduously furthered by the publisher's advertising, which almost kept me from reading the excellent *opusculum*.) Milk, Erich Fromm says, is meant as the quintessence of everything a person requires for allaying the mere needs of life; but honey is the symbol for the sweetness of life and the happiness of existing. And this is precisely what comes across when we are told what the children in the institutions apparently never heard: How good that you exist!

12

Joy Is a By-Product

The happiness of love, lover's bliss, happiness in love, or even *happiness with love*—these are, as everyone knows, fairly ambiguous ideas. In ordinary language they have undergone a rampant growth of meanings, and first of all need a bit of pruning. For the present we shall not go into the question of luck in love, that is, of the good fortune of finding the right partner. That certainly exists, and there is nothing whatsoever to be said against it—although it obviously makes a difference whether what a man is seeking and finding is the woman for the rest of his life ("until death do us part") or what Harvey Cox calls a "Playboy accessory". But we are speaking of something else, of the essential relationship that connects happiness and joy with love, a relationship that, as will become apparent, is not so unequivocal as we might think on first consideration.

Joy is by its nature something secondary and subsidiary. It is of course foolish to ask anyone "why" he wants to rejoice; and so it might be thought that joy is something sought for its

About Love, pp. 72–79, translated by Richard and Clara Winston. © 1974 by Franciscan Herald Press, Chicago. Reprinted with permission.

own sake, and consequently *not* secondary. But if we look into the matter more closely it becomes apparent that man, if all works out as it should, does not want to plunge absolutely and unconditionally into the psychological state of rejoicing but that he wants to have a reason for rejoicing. "If all works out as it should"! For sometimes things do not work out as they should—for example when in the absence of a "reason" a "cause" is brought to bear by a kind of manipulation, a pretext that does not result in real joy but artificially produces a deceptive, unfounded feeling of joy. Such a cause may be a drug or it may be the electric stimulation of certain brain centers. Julian Huxley has argued that "after all, electric happiness is still happiness"; but for the time being I remain convinced that St. Augustine correctly defines the true state of affairs—as well, incidentally, as expressing the viewpoint of the average man—when he says, "There is no one who would not prefer to endure pain with a sound mind than to rejoice in madness." Man can (and wants to) rejoice only when there is a reason for joy. And this reason, therefore, is primary, the joy itself secondary.

But are there not countless reasons for joy? Yes. But they can all be reduced to a common denominator: our receiving or possessing something we love—even though this receiving or possession may only be hoped for as a future good or remembered as something already past. Consequently, one who loves nothing and no one cannot rejoice, no matter how desperately he wishes to (this is the situation in which the temptation to self-deception by constructing "artificial paradises" gains force).

Up to this point the intimate connection between love and joy seems to be a clear, uncomplicated matter. We desire something that we "like" and "love"—and then we receive it as a gift. Something that we tried to bring about by loving effort—we call this "love's labor"—finally succeeds (a scientific proof, the breeding of a new variety of rose, a poem). Then there is the story of the two prisoners of war in Siberia who ask themselves when people are truly happy and what makes them so, and who arrive at the conclusion: being together with those whom they love. In all these examples the link between love and joy is direct and convincing. The much-cited "joy of being loved" is also a relatively clear though not entirely "pure" case—because some alien elements might well adulterate the joy of having someone else say, "How wonderful that you exist" (elements such as gratified vanity, confirmation of status—and so on).

But what about the joy of loving itself, that is, the joy that consists in loving? On the one hand, we have only to have the experience to immediately affirm, "Yes, this joy certainly does exist!" But then how can joy be something secondary, be the response to receiving or possessing something beloved? My answer to this question would be: Because we love to love! In fact we actually are receiving something beloved *by loving*. Our whole being is so set that it wants to be able to say with reason, "How good that this exists; how wonderful that you are here!" The "reason", of course, the only reason that seems cogent to our own minds must be that the existence of those praised things or persons actually *is* "good" and "wonderful". As has already been said, in this is manifested the "solid" aspect of the context of life as a whole: that the indivisibility of love and joy is not a delusion, wherein two separate emotions or physiological stimuli only seem to merge, but is in fact a response to reality—primarily, of course, to the real suitability to one another of human beings who feel "good" toward each other. They were indeed created for one another. Once again we are reminded, in a fresh way, that love has the nature of a gift: not only being loved, but also loving. And the element of gratitude, which is already present in the first stirrings of love, now becomes somewhat more comprehensible. It is gratitude that we are actually receiving what we by nature long for and love: to be able wholeheartedly to "approve" of something, to be able to say that something is good.

We must not allow this perception, which reflects the way
Creation is fundamentally constituted, to be thrust off onto
some innocuous, poetic sidetrack (although on the other hand
Goethe's well-known lines, "Happy alone/Is the soul who
loves" [the last lines of the poem, "Freudvoll und leidvoll"],
are incomparably precise and realistic). Perhaps if we look at
the reverse of the coin we will come to a better understanding
of this difficult matter. The reverse is the inability to love,
fundamental indifference, "the despairing possibility that
nothing matters". The true antithesis of love is not hate, but
despairing indifference, the feeling that nothing is important.

Despair is to be taken here more literally than it might
seem. The radical attitude of "not giving a damn" in fact is in
some way related to the state of mind of the damned. In Dostoevsky's novel *The Brothers Karamazov* Father Zossima says:
"Fathers and teachers, I ponder 'What is hell?' I maintain that
it is the suffering of being unable to love. Once in infinite existence, immeasurable in time and space, a spiritual creature
was given, on his coming to earth, the power of saying, 'I am
and I love'."

Should anyone find this too mystical or too theological,
perhaps he will be more impressed by what a German writer
of these present times, returned home from exile, has to report
concerning his direct experience. Though phrased more personally, it is basically no different from the Russian monk's
wisdom. "During this time I experienced two kinds of happiness", he writes in summing up his feelings upon his return
home. "The one was being able to help, to alleviate suffering.
The other, and perhaps it was the greatest and most blessed
happiness that has ever come my way, was: *Not to have to
hate.*"

But is there not such a thing as "*unhappy* love"? And if so,
what light does that shed upon the seemingly plausible correlation of love and joy?

Let us say, by way of leaping ahead somewhat, that unhappy love not only exists as a fact, but that lovers alone can

be unhappy. "Never are we less protected against suffering than when we love", says Sigmund Freud; and an American psychologist actually calls love itself "an experience of greater vulnerability". This has been known, and expressed, forever and a day; we may find it said in Thomas à Kempis' *Imitatio Christi* and also, of course, in C. S. Lewis' book on love, which we have already quoted several times: "Love anything, and your heart will certainly be wrung and possibly be broken. If you want to make sure of keeping it intact, you must give your heart to no one, not even to an animal." Obviously only a lover can have the experience of not receiving or of losing something loved; and that means being unhappy. Moreover, the failure to receive or the loss can be experienced as something in the present, or it can be remembered, or it can even be anticipated in despair. The inability to mourn rests upon inability to love.

Of course not receiving what we love can occur in a great variety of ways besides the one we are first inclined to think of: unrequited love in which the beloved turns away. The mystics likewise speak of this anguish: God is silent; he does not show himself. They call it "aridity" and "the sterile season". But another possibility is that the beloved being falls upon evil ways and commits wrongs. Then, too, the lover is bound to be unhappy, since loving another means wishing that everything will work out entirely well for the beloved, that the beloved will be "all right", not just happy, but perfect and good.

Then where do we stand? Do both principles apply simultaneously: love and joy belong together, but love and sorrow likewise—just as Thomas Aquinas says with his cool objectivity: *ex amore procedit et gaudium et tristitia*, "out of love comes joy as well as sadness"? Is it a simple matter of both this and that? No, it is not quite so simple.

First: there can of course be love without pain and sorrow, but love without joy is impossible. Second, and this is the main thing: even the unhappy lover is happier than the non-lover, with whom the lover would never change places. In the fact of loving he has already partaken of something beloved. What is more, he still has a share in the beloved who has rejected him, been ungrateful to him, gone astray or in some other way caused him grief. He has that share and keeps it, because the lover in some way remains linked with, remains one with, the beloved. Even unhappy or unrequited love has broken through the principle of isolation on which "the whole philosophy of hell rests" and so has gained a solid basis for joy, a part no matter how small of "paradise".

In the light of this it becomes clearer why so many attempts to define love mention joy as an essential component of the concept. Here I am not thinking principally of that famous or notorious characterization, cast in the form of a geometrical theorem, to be found in the long list of definitions in Spinoza's *Ethics*: "Love is joy with the accompanying idea of an external cause." This is a dubious, not to say disturbing, definition on a number of grounds. Suppose we were playing a guessing game and put this question: What is joy with the accompanying idea of an external cause? Who would ever guess that the answer was supposed to be love? And as a matter of fact Spinoza's definition has run into heavy criticism. Alexander Pfänder remarks that it indicates "very crude psychology" and that "its complete wrongness" is easy to perceive. Schopenhauer goes so far as to cite Spinoza's definition merely "for amusement, because of its extraordinary naiveté". For my own part, I would point out that this "definition" does not even make it apparent that purely in terms of elementary grammar "to love" is a transitive verb, that is to say, a verb that must be linked with a direct object. To love always implies to love *someone* or *something*. And if this element is missing in a definition, it has failed to hit its target.

Leibnitz gives a magnificent characterization of love—and, moreover, in a context in which we would scarcely expect to find it. In his *Codex iuris gentium diplomaticus* he writes, "To love means to rejoice in the happiness of another." But of course we must ask, "But what if the other is not happy?" And later, in his *Nouveaux Essais*, Leibnitz offers a more precise formulation: "To love means to be inclined to rejoice in the perfection, in the goodness or in the happiness of another." That comes very close to the heart of the phenomenon, and does not differ so greatly from the exclamation: How good that you exist!

A century earlier St. Francis de Sales said almost the same thing, although his phraseology is just a shade more exact. Love, he declares in his *Traité de l'amour de Dieu*, is *the* act in which the will unites and joins with the joy and the welfare of someone else.

If we consider our own experience with people, we will in fact realize that shared joy is a more reliable sign of real love than shared grief, or compassion; it is also far more rare. We need not agree with the Duc de La Rochefoucauld's cynical aphorism that there is something not altogether displeasing to us in our best friends' misfortunes. But it is evident that a good many foreign elements having nothing to do with love may be involved in compassion — which, therefore, is not so "pure" a case as shared joy.

Immanual Kant is so constituted that he basically mistrusts everything done out of "inclination", that is, out of joy. To him respect for duty is the only serious moral feeling. ("Man is aware with the greatest clarity that he . . . must completely separate his desire for happiness from the concept of duty.") For Kant "laboriousness" is the standard of all moral values. Yet even Kant is forced to recognize the relationship of love and joy: the fact of the matter is simply too compelling. His firm emphasis on doing as the true proof of love merits attention and respect, and we should not dismiss him too rapidly for his inflexible severity. After all, the New Testament contains some sentences that sound a similar note: "If you love me, you will keep my commandments" (Jn 14:15). And so there is much to be said for Kant's comment: "To love one's neighbor means to do all of one's duty toward him *gladly*."

But what is meant by this *gladly*—the emphasis is Kant's in the *Critique of Practical Reason*? Of course it means nothing less than: with joy.

13

Sex and Despair

There is no need to declare the present "sexualization" of all aspects of public life as simply our fateful destiny; for too much in it is media hyperbole and commercial manipulation.

On the other hand, such "cutting loose" of sexuality as potential human deviation has, of course, been with us since time immemorial, not only as behavior—which we may find easy to understand—but also as doctrine.

This precisely is the background situation, for example, in one of the great and famous Platonic dialogues: a certain Phaedrus crosses Socrates' path, a youth still shocked and under the spell of a meeting he has just attended in which avant-garde intellectuals discussed their convictions. Plato characterizes these intellectuals as people who use pompous arguments to reject traditional norms, who claim to lead an enlightened lifestyle, and who advocate total license for every human impulse. Phaedrus is fascinated by the progressive and elegant tone of a speech given at that meeting by the "greatest author of our era", and he tells Socrates about their "program". Put in a nutshell, it proclaims these propositions: desire should be

Originally published in *Über die Liebe* (Munich: Kösel-Verlag, 1972). Translated by Lothar Krauth.

without love; the aim should be maximal enjoyment with minimal personal engagement; any erotic emotion, the passion of love, is seen as a romantic sickness that needlessly complicates things; and the refusal to accept any deeper commitment is explicitly declared to be the only "reasonable" attitude—indeed, this alone could properly be called "decency", a virtue (*areté*).

It is clear, perhaps surprisingly so, that these propositions sound strikingly contemporary; more specifically, they express attitudes that men are obviously able to formulate and practice at any time in history.

Socrates listens quietly to the gullible Phaedrus and for a time pretends to be equally fascinated and impressed. Then he puts an abrupt end to this game of pretending: "Don't you see, my dear Phaedrus, how shameful all this is? Just imagine a truly noble person had listened to our conversation, someone who is devoted in love to someone else likewise of noble mind. This person would have to presume, would he not, that he had just listened to people raised among galley slaves who have never grasped the true meaning of love among free persons."

Contrary to all appearances, this setting of "free men" against "galley slaves", of course, has nothing at all to do with the realities of a slaveholder society—I think this requires no specific explanation. "Slavery", in this context, indeed means something that no social reform, no "emancipation" could ever overcome; it means, rather, something that can crop up in all social classes, as shown in our example of Athens' upper crust. It means an attitude that in an ethical sense is base and vulgar, and whose façade of civilized refinement nonetheless hides barbaric rudeness and brutality.

What makes this consumer sex without *eros* so ugly and so inhuman is essentially this: it empties the love encounter of its inner significance within the larger framework of human existence, its essence of stepping out from self-centered limitation by opening up to—and becoming one with—another person. As mere partner in *sex*, however, the other is not looked upon as a person, a living human being with an individual human face. An American author has described this reality with the tongue-in-cheek yet accurate observation that from a playboy's point of view the fig leaf has simply been transferred—it now conceals the human face. The man who merely lusts after a woman does not, indeed, really desire "a woman", in spite of the words. True yearning for the beloved, for togetherness with the beloved, springs from what philosophy calls the *eros*. Mere sex, in contrast, desires something impersonal, an object; not a *Thou* but a *thing*: "Just the thing in itself", as the partners in George Orwell's *1984* explicitly assure each other. "Let's do that thing", they say in one of Heinrich Böll's novels. Some speak right to the point of the "deception" in the encounter whose object is only sex. True, for a moment the illusion of "becoming one" may arise; but such an outward union, without love, leaves the two more thoroughly strangers to each other than before. No wonder, then, that "in a society where love is based on sex, where love is not the prerequisite for the gift of physical union", sexuality is paradoxically "separating rather than uniting man and woman, abandoning them to more loneliness and isolation at the very moment when they thought to have surely found the other". The surprise, or better, the disappointment inherent in this paradox—it only seems a paradox, of course—is intensified as sex becomes more and more a commodity available at any time.

Such a result, remarks Paul Ricoeur—loss of value by being readily available—was certainly not anticipated by the generation of Sigmund Freud when those sexual taboos were smashed. "Whatever facilitates the sexual encounter also helps it sink into irrelevance." This should come as no surprise at all. It may well be an absolute principle that anything available "on demand" at almost no cost, and instantly to boot (the Americans use the rugged expression "short-order sex") will necessarily lose not only its value but its attraction as well.

The director of a health center at an American state university, a psychiatrist by profession, relates this experience: promiscuous female students, when questioned, would answer, "It's just too much trouble to say 'no'." At first this may bespeak enormous freedom, but what it really means is more like, "I don't care, it's all the same, it doesn't matter." This premise already contains its inevitable consequence: a sexuality not only lacking joy, but lacking pleasure as well. "So much sex and so little meaning or even fun in it!"

I mentioned that a generally valid principle prevails here. In his later years Goethe once put it this way, though in an entirely different context: "Every century tries to make the sacred vulgar, the difficult easy, the serious hilarious — which really would not be objectionable at all if only earnestness and fun were not both destroyed in the process." Here we have it: the fun gets destroyed, too! And so it is frighteningly appropriate that the above-mentioned experience by that university psychiatrist was published under the title, "The Roots of Student Despair".

14

Fulfillment Means Change

There are, of course, several aspects of the phenomenon known as "love". One such, for example, is friendship, or more exactly, the love of friends. That is in fact a special form of love, though one that nowadays, oddly enough, comes in

About Love, pp. 114–22, translated by Richard and Clara Winston. © 1974 by Franciscan Herald Press, Chicago. Reprinted with permission.

for little praise, whereas Aristotle devoted to it one entire book of the ten books that make up his *Nicomachean Ethics*. Friendship takes time, he says there; it is normally not kindled just by the sight of the other, but by the surprise at discovering that here is someone else who "sees things exactly" the way one sees them oneself, someone of whom one can say happily, "It's good that you exist!" Friends do not gaze at each other, and totally unlike erotic lovers they are not apt to talk about their friendship. Their gaze is fixed upon the things in which they take a common interest. That is why, it has been said, people who simply wish for "a friend" will with fair certainty not find any. To find a friend you first have to be interested in something. Although, therefore, real intimacy does not exist in friendship, a friend is perhaps the only human being in whose presence we speak with complete sincerity and "think aloud" without embarrassment.

So far we also have not spoken directly of the distinctive qualities of maternal love. It has always been said that mothers, as those who love most intensely, seek less to be loved than to love. A mother's love for her children is "unconditional" in a unique fashion; that is, it is not linked with any preconditions. Because of that it corresponds to the deepest longings of children, and indeed of every human being. Maternal love doesn't have to be "earned"; and there is nothing anyone can do to lose it. A father, on the contrary, tends to set conditions; his love has to be earned. But that likewise repeats a fundamental element peculiar to all love: the desire that the beloved not only "feel good" but that things may in truth go well for him. A mature person's love must, as has rightly been remarked, contain both elements, the maternal and the paternal, something unconditional and something demanding.

And so there may well be an untold number of possible ways for human beings to feel good toward one another, to like each other, to feel closeness and affection for one another. But varied as these forms and unsystematic as these degrees of fondness, attachment, liking and solidarity obviously may be, they all have one thing in common with friendship, parental love, fraternity and specifically erotic love: that the lover, turning to the beloved, says, "It's good that you are here; it's wonderful that you exist!" (Unexpectedly we see once more that mere sex partnership cannot be included in this category —because in such partnerships there is no trace of a "you"; there is an ego, and maybe there are two egos, but there is no "you" involved!)

The fundamental affirmation that recurs in identical form in all real love is, as we said at the very beginning of our reflections, by its nature and quite apart from the lovers' awareness of it, the re-enactment of something else that precedes it. It is an imitation of the divine creative act by virtue of which the human being we have just encountered, who suits us and who seems "made for us", exists; by virtue of which, in fact, all reality exists at all and is simultaneously "good", that is, lovable.

But this aspect of the phenomenon of love, which admittedly points beyond empirically knowable reality, must be considered more closely once more—in order for us to be able to name and grasp another special form of love that we have hitherto said nothing about, at any rate not explicitly, but that most certainly cannot be overlooked. Not that we have any intention of going into theology! A theological book on love, that is one interpreting the documents of the sacred tradition and revelation, would undoubtedly have to deal with entirely different matters from those we are now about to discuss. No, we shall keep our eyes fixed upon the phenomenon of love as we encounter it in our experience. The question is, however, whether we may not, by dint of including in our considerations something that belongs to the realm of belief, be able to clarify and interpret a fact of experience that would otherwise remain obscure and uncomprehended.

There is, for example, to pitch our discussion in concrete terms at once, the quite empirical contemporary phenomenon of Mother Teresa, the Yugoslav nun in Calcutta who has recently been receiving a considerable amount of publicity. She taught English literature in her order's high school for girls. One day she could no longer endure seeing, on her way to school, deathly ill and dying people lying in the street without receiving any humane aid. She therefore persuaded the city government to let her have an empty, neglected pilgrims' rest house and in it established her subsequently famous Hospital for the Dying. I have seen this shelter, which at the beginning was a most dismal place. Of course people die inside it likewise—but now they need no longer perish amidst the bustle of the streets. They feel something of the presence of a sympathetic person.

On the one hand what can we call this work of mercy but a form of loving concern, nourished by the fundamental impulse of "It's good that you exist" and affecting the loving person not just on a supernatural or spiritual level detached from all natural emotions. Rather, it affects him through all the levels of his being. *On the other hand* something new and fundamentally different is taking place here, or at any rate something that cannot so easily be reduced to a common denominator with friendship, liking, fondness, being smitten—and so on.

I should like to try, step by step, to make this new element seem plausible, to show how it is something lying within man's potential, or more precisely, something that has been put within the scope of human feeling. The first step, without our knowing it, has already been taken. It consists in our reenacting, whenever we love, the primal affirmation that took place in the Creation. But it would also be possible that —taking the second step—we "realize" deliberately this iterative aspect of our loving. When we find something we see good, glorious, wonderful (a tree; the structure of a diatom seen under the microscope; above all, of course, a human face, a friend, one's partner for the whole of life, but also one's own existence in the world) — when we see something good, I say, when we love something lovable, we might become aware of our actually taking up and continuing that universal approval of the Creation by which all that has been created is "loved by God" and is therefore good. It would be a further step, beyond the mere recognition of this truth, to wish to observe it expressly, as if we were joining in with the Creator's affirmative and allying ourselves with it in a sort of identification — joining with the primordial act of affirmation and also with the "Actor". We might, in other words, for our part also love the "First Lover". Obviously that would change our own love for things and people, especially for those whom one loves more than all others; our own love, that is, would receive a wholly new and literally absolute confirmation. And the beloved, though still altogether incomparable, still someone personally and specially intended for us, would at the same time suddenly appear as one point of light in an infinite mesh of light.

Yet even after we had taken this step, we would still not have attained the stage of *caritas* and *agapé* in the strict sense. The true motives of that remarkable nun in Calcutta would not yet have come into view. Incidentally, when a reporter remarked to her in astonishment that he would not do "anything like that" if he were paid a thousand dollars a day for it, she is said to have replied, tersely and magnificently, "Neither would I." Anyone who seriously asked her, "Why are you doing this?" would probably receive the reply — if she did not choose to remain silent — "For the sake of Christ!" At this point Anders Nygren is undeniably right; love in the form of *agapé* is "the original basic conception of Christianity". It rests upon the certain faith that the event which in the language of theology is called "Incarnation" conferred upon man the gift of an immediate and real participation in God's creative power of affirmation. Or as we might also put it: participation in the divine love, which is what creates the being as well as the goodness of the world in the first place. As a consequence of that man can turn to another person in a way that otherwise he would be utterly incapable of doing and, while remaining altogether himself, can say to that other, "It's good that you are." And it is precisely this more intensive force of approval, operating from a wholly fresh basis, that is intended by the word *caritas* (*agapé*). But because like God's own love it is universal, at least in intention, excluding nothing and no one, we find we can use the word meaningfully without explicitly naming an object, saying for example that someone is "in love" (1 Jn 4:18). Such love, no matter how "forlorn" it may seem, possesses that imperturbable non-irritability of which the New Testament speaks: *caritas non irritatur* (1 Cor 13:5). Likewise other hyperboles, such as that in love a maximum of freedom is attained and that it gives the heart perfect peace, prove true only with regard to *caritas*.

It is really self-evident that the images hitherto employed, of a succession of steps and stages, do not quite accord with the radical newness and otherness of that participation in the creative love of God which has been given to man—what in the New Testament is called Grace. Nevertheless, the great tradition of Christendom has always insisted that this new thing is indeed tied to what man is by nature and by virtue of creation with an inseparable, though almost indescribable, bond.

Above all, *caritas* in the Christian sense does not invalidate any of the love and affirmation which we are able to feel on our own, and which frequently we do feel as a matter of course. Rather, *caritas* comprehends all the forms of human love. For after all it is our own natural, native will, kindled at the Creation and by virtue of this very origin tempestuously demanding appeasement, that is now exalted to immediate participation in the will of the Creator himself—and therefore necessarily presupposed.

Anyone who considers and accepts this principle cannot find it surprising that the whole conception of *caritas* is dominated by felicity. If happiness is truly never anything but happiness in love, then the fruit of that highest form of love must be the utmost happiness, for which language offers such names as felicity, beatitude, bliss. Nor should this be in any way confused with "eudemonism". In the first place felicity means not so much the subjective feeling of happiness as the objective, existential appeasement of the will by the *bonum universale*, by the quintessence of everything for which our whole being hungers and which we are capable of longing for in (only seemingly paradoxical) "selfless self-love". Moreover, felicity, as has already been said, cannot be defined positively at all in regard to its content; it is a *bonum ineffabile*, toward which our love ultimately directs itself, a good that cannot be grasped in words.

At any rate, although we may find the fact startling and troublesome at first, the great teachers of Christendom always considered the concepts of *caritas* and felicity as very closely linked. "*Caritas* is not just any kind of love of God, but a love for God that loves him as the object and the author of happiness." And in the world, we are told, we can love in the mode of *caritas* only what is capable of sharing happiness, or beatitude, with us. This includes our bodies, into which happiness will "flood back"; but above all our fellow men, insofar as they will be our companions in beatitude (or ought to be).

Of course it is possible to ask skeptically just what it means to love another as the possible companion of future beatitude. Would love of this sort alter matters at all? I think that in fact a great deal would be altered if we succeeded in regarding another person (whether friend, beloved, son, neighbor, adversary and rival or even an unknown who needed our help) truly as one destined like ourselves to share in the perfection of bliss, as our *socius in participatione beatudinis*. That other person would then, in my view, simply enter into a new dimension of reality. From one moment to the next we would realize that "there are no ordinary people".

It is no accident that almost all the above has been written in the conditional tense, the *modus irrealis*. In fact it happens very seldom, and only to a few persons, to see the extraordinariness of everyone ("wonderfully created and even more wonderfully re-created"), let alone to respond to it with the exclamation of love: It's wonderful that you are! This is, as we see, not so very far from the vocabulary of *eros*. And truly, if anyone has asked what in the world the mutual rapture of lovers has to do with the work of a nun who wishes to succor dying beggars—precisely this is the point at which the hidden common element becomes visible, as if seen through a tiny crack.

It also becomes immediately apparent that the act of *caritas* is not simply a further step on the road of *eros*, and that what is involved is something different from mere "sublimation". It is true that *caritas* can be incorporated into the most commonplace forms of expression in men's dealings with their fellows. In fact, that is usually what will be done with it—so that possibly, to the uninitiated eye, there will be scarcely anything noticeable about its outward appearance to set it off from the usual conduct of people reasonably well disposed toward one another. In other words, the natural forms of love are presupposed to be intact; and no special, solemnly sublime vocabulary is needed to describe the operations of *caritas*. Still, the classical statement of the relationship of Grace and Nature speaks not only of presupposition and intactness, but also of the perfecting of what man by nature is and has. And when I said that the bond between *eros* and *caritas* exists but is almost indescribable, the difficulty of description in practice consists in this question: What is the meaning of "perfecting"? This is one of those concepts which probably can never be known and defined before it is experienced. It is simply in the nature of the thing that the apprentice can have no specific idea of what the perfection of mastery looks like from inside, and all that is going to demand of him. Perfection always includes transformation. And transformation necessarily means parting from what must be overcome and abandoned precisely for the sake of preserving identity in change.

"Perfection" in *caritas*, therefore, may very well mean that *eros*, in order to keep its original impulse and remain really love, above all in order to attain the "foreverness" that it naturally desires, must transform itself altogether, and that this transformation perhaps resembles passing through something akin to dying. Such thoughts are, at any rate, not unfamiliar to mankind's reflections on love. *Caritas*, in renewing and rejuvenating us, also brings us death in a certain sense: *facit in nobis quamdam mortem*, says Augustine. The same thing is conveyed by the familiar figure of speech which calls *caritas*, because it consumes everything and transforms everything into itself, a fire.

Thus it is much more than an innocuous piety when Christendom prays, "Kindle in us the fire of thy love."

15

The Art of Making the Right Decisions

Highest in rank among the four cardinal virtues is *prudence*—a notion quite alien to us, if indeed we find any meaning in it at all. And I have not even used a precise formulation yet! Prudence, strictly speaking, does not stand on the same level as *justice, courage,* and *temperance*; she is not, as it were, the eldest or the most beautiful of the four sisters. Prudence—to stay with this image—is rather the mother of the other virtues, the *genitrix virtutum*, the virtue bearer, in the words of Thomas Aquinas. This means, expressed without the image, that justice, courage and temperance exist only because of prudence! Prudence is the precondition for all that is ethically good.

What stands in our way of ready understanding is the actual current usage of the word "prudence", which may even mean some sort of cleverness in getting around ethical goodness. ("Do you think he'd stand up for his convictions? He's much too prudent for that!") But I will leave aside this linguistic aspect for now. Let us consider the question of what the ancient maxim really means by its assertion that a person is always and necessarily one *and* the other, both prudent *and* virtuous; even more precisely: that first comes prudence and then, because of it, virtue. What this means is really not far removed from our everyday thinking and speaking. It means that to do

"Die Aktualität der Kardinaltugenden", originally published in *Buchstabier-Übungen* (Munich: Kösel-Verlag, 1980). Translated by Lothar Krauth.

what in reality is right and good presupposes some knowledge about reality; if you do not know how it is with things and how they stand, you are *in concreto* (practically) unable to choose what is ethically good. The mere "good intention", the desire to be just, for instance, does not suffice at all.

To recognize what is real, however, should certainly not be thought an easy endeavor; it is quite exacting and in many ways hazardous. Goethe once wrote: "In all actions and decisions it is important to perceive clearly the objects involved and to deal with them according to their nature." All very well! But these objects never appear as neutral entities in some disinterested perception of "reality"; these very objects envelop and make up the situation that demands our decision; they form precisely the bluntly concrete circumstance here and now that stands in constant flux and that we perceive, as a rule, according to the lights of our own very personal interests. What is asked of us, then, is no less than this: to reduce our own interest to that silence which is an absolute precondition if we want to hear or perceive anything. Yet everybody knows—whether we are dealing with the reconstruction of a traffic accident or trying to arrive at an adequate judgment in some dispute: Should one of the parties involved fail to see the events the way they really occurred, then all further considerations become futile; the precondition for further reasoning is simply missing. The precondition for *every* ethical decision is the perception and examination of reality. And yet this perception makes up only the first half of prudence; the other half consists in "translating" our knowledge of reality into decision and action. We are thus able to state: prudence is the art of making the right decision based on the corresponding reality—no matter whether justice, courage or temperance is at stake.

Here the question may arise: Is this not asking too much of the average person? My answer is twofold. First: our knowledge of reality is by its nature the result of a communal endeavor. It is still true, of course, that ultimately only the autonomous individual, the morally defined person, stands under the call and the obligation to make decisions, and this responsibility cannot be delegated. Yet the individual, in acquiring knowledge of reality, is dependent on the other person. This is the reason that the ancient sages invariably considered receptivity to teaching, the willingness to accept advice, an essential element in the virtue of prudence. This receptivity to advice, while remaining subject to the determination by the individual, the morally acting person, must never be misled and deceived. In other words: it becomes evident in this context how important the presence of truth in public discourse is or, negatively, how important the public manipulation of reality is (for instance, through the deceptive use of language and communication), not only for society at large but also for every decision-making individual.

Now the second part of my answer to the question of whether the call to prudence may not be asking too much of the average person: to be prudent is not the equivalent of being "highly educated" or "learned". A certain kind of "wisdom", though, is indispensable in prudence; a wisdom that can be elicited from anybody, meaning a form of dispassionate objectivity as expressed in this play on words that was a commonplace for centuries in Europe: *cui sapiunt omnia prout sunt, hic est vere sapiens*, that is, to savor all things as they really are is truly to taste wisdom.

16

Being—Truth—Good

The structural framework of Western Christian metaphysics as a whole stands revealed, perhaps more plainly than in any other single ethical dictum, in the proposition that prudence is the foremost of the virtues. That structure is built thus: that Being precedes Truth, and that Truth precedes the Good. Indeed, the living fire at the heart of the dictum is the central mystery of Christian theology: that the Father begets the Eternal Word, and that the Holy Spirit proceeds out of the Father and the Word.

Since this is so, there is a larger significance in the fact that people today can respond to this assertion of the pre-eminence of prudence only with incomprehension and uneasiness. That they feel it as strange may well reveal a deeper-seated and more total estrangement. It may mean that they no longer feel the binding force of the Christian Western view of man. It may denote the beginning of an incomprehension of the fundamentals of Christian teaching in regard to the nature of reality.

The Four Cardinal Virtues, pp. 3–4, translated by Richard and Clara Winston. © 1954, 1955, 1959 by Pantheon Books, Inc.; © 1965 by Harcourt Brace Jovanovich, Inc. Reprinted by permission of Harcourt Brace Jovanovich.

17

"Doing the Truth"

Prudence, then, is the mold and mother of all virtues, the circumspect and resolute shaping power of our minds which transforms knowledge of reality into realization of the good. It holds within itself the humility of silent, that is to say, of unbiased perception; the trueness-to-being of memory; the art of receiving counsel; alert, composed readiness for the unexpected. Prudence means the studied seriousness and, as it were, the filter of deliberation, and at the same time the brave boldness to make final decisions. It means purity, straightforwardness, candor, and simplicity of character; it means standing superior to the utilitarian complexities of mere "tactics".

Prudence is, as Paul Claudel says, the "intelligent prow" of our nature which steers through the multiplicity of the finite world toward perfection.

In the virtue of prudence the ring of the active life is rounded out and closed, is completed and perfected; for man, drawing on his experience of reality, acts in and upon reality, thus realizing himself in decision and in act. The profundity of this concept is expressed in the strange statement of Thomas Aquinas that in prudence, the commanding virtue of the "conduct" of life, the happiness of active life is essentially comprised.

The Four Cardinal Virtues, p. 22, translated by Richard and Clara Winston. © 1954, 1955, 1959 by Pantheon Books, Inc.; © 1965 by Harcourt Brace Jovanovich, Inc. Reprinted by permission of Harcourt Brace Jovanovich.

Prudence is that illumination of moral existence which, according to one of the wisest books of the East, is a thing denied to every man who "looks at himself".

There is a gloomy type of resoluteness, and a bright type. Prudence is the brightness of the resoluteness of that man who "does the truth" (Jn 3:21).

18

The Prudence of Love

In the *Summa theologica* we learn that upon a higher plane of perfection—that is, the plane of charity—there is also a higher and extraordinary prudence which holds as nought all the things of this world.

Does this not run completely counter to all that the "universal teacher" has said elsewhere about the nature of the first cardinal virtue? Is holding created things as nought not the exact opposite of that reverent objectivity which in the concrete situation of concrete action must attempt to recognize the "measure" of that action?

Things are nought only before God, who created them and in whose hand they are as clay in the hand of the potter. By the superhuman force of grace-given love, however, man may become one with God to such an extent that he receives,

The Four Cardinal Virtues, pp. 38–40, translated by Richard and Clara Winston. © 1954, 1955, 1959 by Pantheon Books, Inc.; © 1965 by Harcourt Brace Jovanovich, Inc. Reprinted by permission of Harcourt Brace Jovanovich.

so to speak, the capacity and the right to see created things from God's point of view and to "relativize" them and see them as nought from God's point of view, *without* at the same time repudiating them or doing injustice to their nature. Growth in love is the legitimate avenue and the one and only justification for "contempt for the world".

Unlike this contempt which arises out of growth in love, all contempt for the world which springs from man's own judgment and opinions, not from the supernatural love of God, is simple arrogance, hostile to the nature of being; it is a form of pride in that it refuses to recognize the ordinary obligations which are made visible to man in created things. Only that closer union with the being of God which is nourished by love raises the blessed man beyond immediate involvement in created things.

At this point in our argument we approach a limit. Beyond that limit only the experience of the saints can offer any valid knowledge, any valid comment. We would only remind our readers how intensely the great saints loved the ordinary and commonplace, and how anxious they were lest they might have been deceived into regarding their own hidden craving for the "extraordinary" as a "counsel" of the Holy Spirit of God.

But even in that higher and extraordinary form of prudence which holds the world in contempt, there reigns unrestrictedly the same fundamental attitude upon which ordinary prudence entirely depends: the fundamental attitude of justice toward the being of things and correspondence to reality.

The eye of perfected friendship with God is aware of deeper dimensions of reality, to which the eyes of the average man and the average Christian are not yet opened. To those who have this greater love of God the truth of real things is revealed more plainly and more brilliantly; above all, the supernatural reality of the Trinitarian God is made known to them more movingly and overwhelmingly.

Even supreme supernatural prudence, however, can have only the following aim: to make the more deeply felt truth of the reality of God and world the measure for will and action. Man can have no other standard and signpost than things as they are and the truth which makes manifest things as they are; and there can be no higher standard than the God who is and his truth.

19

"We Have a Holy Sovereign"

Whoever considers the notion of "justice" nowadays, especially young people, may feel prompted at once, indeed challenged, to think of "society" as well. "Society" may be perceived as the embodiment of injustice—perhaps not altogether a misconstruing. We must remind ourselves, however, that our reflection here regards justice as a *virtue*, namely, an attitude to be achieved by the individual, even expected from the individual and the individual alone. Justice has been called the art of "getting along"—a formulation equally open to misunderstanding, as though it meant nothing more than some mutually acceptable accommodation. This, of course, is not the true meaning of "justice". We can speak of justice when each person in a group is accorded his rightful due: "To each his own", as the ancient expression goes. This precisely describes justice in the tradition of European thought, from the ancient

Originally published in *Menschliches Richtigsein* (Freiburg im Breisgau: Informationszentrum Berufe der Kirche, 1980). Translated by Lothar Krauth.

Greeks to the social encyclicals of the popes: the habitual disposition of the will to render each and all we encounter their rightful due.

The concept of justice, then, as is easily seen, contains one other dimension; it presupposes something that is different from justice as such: it presupposes someone who is entitled to something, and it presupposes also that the one who is called to exercise justice acknowledges such entitlement.

The question, however, of why indeed, and based on what, those others (and of course I myself, too) can be entitled to certain things, and what therefore has to be given or at least spared them (and me) — this question has no ready answer. It is relatively easy to argue that a worker is entitled to just wages, but even this, in an era that knows forced labor camps, is no longer so self-evident as it may seem. Where, then, may we discover the fundamental reason that everyone endowed with a human face is unconditionally entitled to certain things, simply as a human being — for example: that my dignity as a person be respected? In fact, the decisive concept here is that of "person" — insofar as a person is defined as an autonomous being existing essentially to achieve self-development and self-actualization. And yet, in extremes, when pushed to the limits, such recourse to the concept of "person" alone will not suffice (contrary to the opinions of some noble-minded philosophers). Then we must be able to invoke some absolute authority that stands beyond any human discussion; in other words, each and all human beings are inviolable because I see them, in their essence, as persons created by God.

We should not assume this to be a specifically Christian or even theological conception. A member of the UNESCO commission for the redefinition of human rights, a Chinese and an adherent of Confucianism, explained to his colleagues, probably to their amazement, that the foundation for human rights, in his tradition, is summed up thus: "Heaven loves the people; and the one who governs must obey heaven." And Immanuel Kant, not exactly a Christian philosopher either, declares: "We have a holy Sovereign; what he has given as holy to us humans, these are our human rights."

The fundamental rationale for all power is to safeguard and to protect these rights. Whether we consider political power or authority in more confined situations—in the family, on the job, in a military unit—the following always proves true: whenever such power is not exercised to safeguard justice, dreadful iniquity will result. No calamity causes more despair in this world than the unjust exercise of power. And yet any power that could never be abused is ultimately no power at all—a fearful thought!

If we persist in pushing our reflection still further, we catch sight of one feature that makes our topic of "justice" radically more complicated. The realm of our human relations is such that in certain highly significant situations it becomes impossible actually to render to the other what is doubtless his due. The ancient thinkers here recalled first of all our relationship with God to whom we could never ever say, "Now we are even", meaning, "Now I have rendered you your due." For this reason Christianity's great teachers have declared that our relationship with God could not possibly be marked by justice, and that in its place, almost as a substitute and makeshift, there had to be *religio*: devotion, worship, sacrifice, a penitent heart.

But even in our human relationships lie certain debts that by their very nature can never truly be repaid and absolved. Thus, strictly speaking, I can never render what is their due to my mother, to my teachers, to honest public officials. And to come right down to it, I cannot really "repay" even a friendly waiter or a reliable domestic in such a way that everything I owe them is rendered. Once again, assuming fair and fortunate circumstances, some other virtue is called to substitute whenever justice proves inadequate: reverence, honor and such respect (not only internal respect) as to proclaim: I owe you something I am unable to repay; and I let you know hereby that I am aware of this.

Once we thus acknowledge ourselves to be debtors and recipients in relation to others and to God, we may be reluctant to base our life simply on the selfish question: "What is my due?"

20

"Restitution"

It is not easy to exhaust the implications of the proposition in the *Summa theologica* which says: the act of justice which orders the association of individuals with one another is *restitutio*, recompense, restoration. A French translation tends to weaken what Thomas has said and makes an interpretative insertion to the effect that it is not a question of *the* act of commutative justice but of its principal act (*acte premier*). However, the sense of even this interpretation is that in the field of *iustitia commutativa* "restitution" occupies a unique place. As a matter of fact there is nothing about any other act in Thomas.

What, then, is *restitutio*? Thomas himself gives the answer. "It is seemingly the same as once more (*iterato*) to re-instate a person in the possession or dominion of his thing." It is, then, a *re*-storation, a *re*-compense, a *re*-turning. What are we to make of these reiterations? I think we would lose insight into the meaning hidden here if we were to reduce *restitutio* simply to its present significance of restitution, that is, of returning

The Four Cardinal Virtues, pp. 78–80, translated by Lawrence E. Lynch. © 1954, 1955, 1959 by Pantheon Books, Inc.; © 1965 by Harcourt Brace Jovanovich, Inc. Reprinted by permission of Harcourt Brace Jovanovich.

another person's property and making reparation for some il-
legally wrought injury. Rather, we are here concerned with
"surprise" formulations that point to some unexpressed
thought which is self-evident to Thomas but not to us. A key
to what is meant here can be found in such a familiar phrase
as: "To give to each his own." There is something very much
to the point in Schopenhauer's objection: "If it is his own,
there is no need to *give* it to him." A condition of justice is the
startling fact that a man may *not* have what is nonetheless "his
own"—as the very concept of "something due a person" implies. Consequently, the recognition of the *suum* can rightly be
called re-storation, a re-stitution, re-compense, re-instate-
ment to an original right. And this does not apply only to
cases like theft, fraud, and robbery (Thomas speaks of *commu-
tationes involuntariae*, changes in original ownership which take
place against the will of one of the partners). It is not only in
this area that it is meaningful to speak of *restitutio*; wherever
one man owes another something (even in such voluntary obligations as buying, renting, or borrowing) or wherever due
respect is shown and due thanks are expressed, to give what
is due is always "restitution".

The state of equilibrium that properly corresponds to man's
essence, to his original, "paradisiac" state, is constantly
thrown out of balance, and has constantly to be "restored"
through an act of justice. Nor must the disturbance be necessarily understood as injustice, though the fact that the act of
justice is called *restitutio* presupposes that injustice is the prev-
alent condition in a world dominated by opposing interests,
the struggle for power, and hunger. To bring solace and order
into the conflict of contending interests which by their nature
are legitimate opposites and not easily reconcilable, to impose
on them, as it were, a posterior order, is the office and task of
commutative justice. The establishment of equity has as its
premise that there is no natural equality, or that it exists not
yet, or no longer. That man, especially, is just who does not
become inured and hardened to disorder, not even to a disor-

der he may have originated himself at first impulse (to become a man means learning to be unjust, says Goethe). The just man recognizes when wrong has been done, admits his own injustice, and endeavors to eradicate it. Who would deny that we touch here the sore spot in all reciprocal relationships, and that the basic way to realize commutative justice does in fact have the character of restitution?

Yet, as has already been said, we need not turn our attention only to compensation for injustice. Man's every act "disturbs" the stable equilibrium, since every act turns the doer into either a debtor or a creditor. And since men are constantly becoming indebted to one another, the demand is constantly raised to pay that debt by an act of "restitution". Therefore, the equality that characterizes justice cannot be finally and definitely established at any one time, it cannot be arrested. It must, rather, be constantly re-established, "restored anew" (*iterato*). It has to be "reinstated". The "return to equilibrium", which, Thomas says, occurs in *restitutio*, is an unending task. This means that the dynamic character of man's communal life finds its image within the very structure of every act of justice. If the basic act of commutative justice is called "*re*-stitution", the very word implies that it is never possible for men to realize an ideal and definitive condition. What it means is, rather, that the fundamental condition of man and his world is provisory, temporary, nondefinitive, tentative, as is proved by the "patchwork" character of all historical activity, and that, consequently, any claim to erect a definitive and unalterable order in the world must of necessity lead to something inhuman.

21

The "Common Good"
and What It Means

"Distributive justice regards the allotment of certain things to the individual, insofar as the property of the community also belongs to each member." This means: the "allotment" consists of the individual's share in the *bonum commune* (the common good).

At this point we ought to attempt a clearer description of the *bonum commune*. A preliminary approach may suggest the following definition: the *bonum commune* is the sum total of society's production, the whole of its output. The correct nature of this statement is based on the fact that all social groups and professions, and in rather unstructured, unsystematic ways the individuals as well, function together, thus making available for the people, for the society as a whole, food, clothing, shelter, transportation, communication, health care, training and schools, also the manifold means of pleasure and entertainment. The strict interpretation of *iustitia distributiva* (distributive justice) would require that all these goods and services be distributed and "allotted" evenly among all the members of society. This conception, however, is inadequate.

Such a definition springs from the mentality of a technical mind set that believes that everything can be "made". Because of these roots, such a definition incurs the risk of neglecting

---

Originally published in *Über die Gerechtigkeit* (Munich: Kösel-Verlag, 1953). Translated by Lothar Krauth.

the truth that the *bonum commune* extends beyond the realm of the merely material and usable goods of production. There exist contributions to the common good that are neither "usable" nor "makable" but that nevertheless are quite real and indispensable to boot. This is the meaning of the statement, for example, that it is necessary for the perfection of a commonwealth that there be persons dedicated to contemplation. This states, really, that the life even of society as such is nourished by the public presence of truth and that the life of nations becomes all the richer the more they attain a sense and awareness of the depths of reality.

We should notice here, incidentally, a primary characteristic of the absolute labor State: there the principle prevails of identifying the common good with the "common usefulness", and the plans by which the *bonum commune* allegedly is pursued are all utilitarian in nature.

The second objection to the definition of the *bonum commune* as society's output focuses on a more essential, deeper-rooted deficiency.

The original literal and inherent meaning of *bonum commune* concerns "the good", the essence of all the different goods that together form a community's reason for existing and that a commonwealth would have to achieve and obtain before it could be deemed to have realized its full potential. It appears to me, though, to be definitely *not* possible to define the *bonum commune*, in this sense, with any comprehensiveness and finality. For this would presuppose that it is possible to describe, accurately and definitively, the full potential of a community and therefore its "essence". It is as impossible to formulate this as it is to define the "essence" of the human person—and so nobody is able to state ultimately what constitutes the good of the human person, either—that good, namely, which provides the reason for human existence and which would have to be achieved in life before any human person could be deemed to have realized his full potential. No other meaning than this attaches to Socrates' stubbornly propounded contention that he did not know what "human virtue" was and that he had not yet met anybody who could teach him.

If the *bonum commune* is to be conceived in this way, what, then, does it mean to "render each and all their due"? What does it mean, then, to exercise "distributive justice"? It means: to make sure that the individual members of the population are given the opportunity to add their contribution to the realization of the *bonum commune* that is neither specifically nor comprehensively defined. This participation according to each person's *dignitas* or capacity and ability—this is precisely each person's rightful "due". And this participation may not be prevented by the administrator of the *bonum commune* if the *iustitia distributiva*, the justice of power, is not to be violated. This points to a further aspect: the "good of a commonwealth" includes the inborn human talents, qualities and potentials, and part of the *iustitia distributiva* is the obligation to protect, preserve and foster these capacities.

After all this we are able to identify once again an essential element of totalitarian regimes. There the political powers claim the right to define in complete detail the specifics of the *bonum commune*. The fateful and destructive nature of those five-year plans does not come from their attempt to increase industrial output or to gear production and demand toward each other. What is so ruinous here is the fact that the "plan" becomes the exclusive standard that dictates not only the production of material goods but equally the pursuits of universities, the creations of artists, even the leisure activities of the individual—so that anything not totally conforming to this standard is suppressed as "socially unimportant" and "undesirable".

22

The Power of Evil

[The German playwright] Bertolt Brecht once remarked, "When I hear that a ship needs heroes for a crew I wonder whether the ship is old and unsafe." He has a point. But Bertolt Brecht presumably was not aware of the fact that 1,500 years earlier St. Augustine had said something quite similar; in his book on the City of God we read: "Courage is a testimony to the existence and power of evil in the world." In other words: because justice and goodness do *not* automatically prevail on their own, because on the contrary their success depends on human effort, therefore courage is to be counted among the elements that make a person "right". It is a liberal illusion to assume that you can consistently act justly without ever incurring risks: risks for your immediate well-being, the tranquillity of your daily routine, your possessions, your good name, your public honor—in extreme instances possibly even more: liberty, health and life itself. All this clarifies at the outset some essential features of courage. For instance (as Thomas Aquinas put it), "the praise of courage depends on the justice involved"—notice how carefully this establishes an order of priorities. And this means that anybody who knowingly fights on the side of injustice cannot truly be called courageous; the "courage" of the criminal is indeed a misnomer.

"Die Aktualität der Kardinaltugenden", originally published in *Buchstabier-Übungen* (Munich: Kösel-Verlag, 1980). Translated by Lothar Krauth.

In 1934 I published a small volume on courage and prefaced it with the motto, "The praise of courage depends on the justice involved." My friends at the time knew exactly what I tried to say, and my less friendly contemporaries [the German Nazis] knew it as well.

In addition, it became evident (so I hope) that recklessness, adventurism, bravery, fearlessness, aggression all differ from the concept of courage, which ranks among the four cardinal virtues and thus is declared an essential component of a person's wholeness. Images of risky mountain climbing or dangerous ski jumping are exactly what do *not* illustrate the nature of courage as virtue (contrary to such an attempt by a television program some time ago). How else could this virtue be the call and challenge of all people, of any average person —indeed, of you and me? Invariably, such courage in action is altogether unpretentious. To be courageous means: to oppose injustice in the face of overwhelming external power and to accept willingly any resulting disadvantage, be it only public ridicule or social isolation. In fact, the ultimate proof of courage may very well be marked by the total absence of anything spectacular. Whenever there is talk of daring and braving and risking, we may consider this an almost certain indication that true courage is not present. If a pornographic novel is advertised as "risqué", then in truth nothing at all is being risked. It would be much more risqué to declare publicly that chastity is part of what makes a person whole; this would be much more dangerous. The symbolic figure for courage is indeed not the imposing "hero" and "conqueror" but the martyr, and he is recognized as a martyr only *post factum*. The moment of his ultimate testimony sees him defeated, ridiculed, abandoned and above all: silenced. For this reason the ancient sages declared the decisive element in courage to be endurance, not attack—in a world whose natural inner structure includes the fact of not being "right" on its own.

23

Courage Does Not Exclude Fear

The concept of "courage" does not equate with the notion of aggressive fearlessness at any price. There exists indeed a kind of fearlessness that is the direct opposite of courage. To clarify this thought we have to reflect on the proper place of fear within the framework of human existence.

The superficial "discourse" of everyday life, as a rule, tends to be reassuring, trying as it does to deny the reality of the fearful, or at least to banish it into the realm of mere appearances and imaginations.

This soothing reassurance has been effective—as well as ineffective—at all times. In our own era, however, we witness a remarkable counterpoint to it: in more profound modern writings—in philosophy, psychology, poetry—there appears to be no concept more relevant than that of "anxiety". And one other counterpoint to that trivial reassurance about human existence has sprung up: a new stoicism. It is proclaimed, especially by a circle of men who remember both world wars, as the manifestation of that sort of destruction which promises and threatens further and even more horrible apocalyptic catastrophes. They say that human existence everywhere induces fear, but nothing is so fearful that the strong cannot bear and endure it with dignity. And yet, reading the more intimate writings of someone like Ernst Jünger, for instance, one

Originally published in *Über das christliche Menschenbild* (Munich: Kösel-Verlag, 1964). Translated by Lothar Krauth.

of the outstanding representatives of this new stoicism, one has to conclude that almost all the dreams of these "heroic hearts" are nightmares. Here it should be noted that to register this fact with any kind of satisfaction, or to gloat over its irony would be utterly preposterous. Rather, we should admit that those nightmares could well be a more genuine and probably more adequate reaction to the true metaphysical situation of the Western world than a Christian attitude that is complacently wrapped in the rather superficial security of "cultural" achievements and has not yet plumbed its own depths. These depths conceal the ultimate Christian answer for the matter at hand: the notion of *fear of the Lord*. The popular Christian mentality has virtually transformed this concept into something empty, unreal and abstruse. Fear of the Lord is not simply the same as "respect" toward Almighty God but means a true fear in the narrow sense of the word. There is a common dimension in all fear, anxiety, dread, horror and terror—all are reactions to the various possibilities of existential diminishment, the most extreme of which would be outright obliteration.

Christian theology is far from denying the fearful element in human existence. Equally, a Christian rule of life will never teach that we should not or must not be afraid of the fear-inducing. As Christians, however, we concern ourselves with the *ordo timoris*, the relative importance of different kinds of fear; we reflect on what might be truly and ultimately fearful; we take care not to fear things that are not truly and ultimately fearful, and to fear things that are. The ultimate fearful reality, however, is none other than the possibility that we may sever ourselves, willingly and culpably, from the very source of our being. The possibility of incurring guilt is the ultimate existential threat for every person. It is this ever-present fearful possibility of culpable separation from our source of being to which the fear of the Lord is the adequate response. Human guilt is the ultimate fear-inducing reality; no one could ever be prepared to accept and endure "with dignity" such a fearful thing. This dimension of fear attaches to every human existence as a very real possibility, and even the saints are no exception. No "heroism" whatsoever is able to conquer this dimension, this fear; on the contrary: such fear is the premise for all true heroism. Fear of the Lord—as real fear—must be lived and endured until the final "safety" of eternal life is reached. If courage keeps us from loving our life in such a way as to cause us to lose it—then we understand that fear of the Lord, namely, the fear of losing *eternal* life, is the foundation of all Christian courage. We have to realize, however, that fear of the Lord is but the lesser converse of trusting love of the Lord. St. Augustine says it: we fear what our love runs away from.

Fear of the Lord is the "perfection" of our natural dread of existential diminishment and obliteration. All ethical values are indeed nothing else but some sort of "extension" of natural essential tendencies. It is rooted in human *nature* to dread nothingness, which means: even before and outside any conscious reflection. And this means: residing in the God-given essence of the human person.

The natural tendency to gather together is perfected in the virtue of justice. The natural tendency to assert oneself is perfected in the virtue of magnanimity. The natural tendency to seek pleasure is perfected in the virtue of temperance. And so, too, is the natural fear of obliteration perfected in the fear of the Lord. Just as the natural tendencies to assemble, prevail, and enjoy will turn destructive unless they are refined and perfected into justice, magnanimity and temperance, so also will the natural dread of obliteration become destructive unless it is refined and perfected into fear of the Lord.

In its essential reality as "filial" fear, fear of the Lord is a gift of the Holy Spirit, not the natural moral perfection of a natural human potentiality like the cardinal virtues. It follows from this observation that only a life truly guided by supernatural perfection has the power to liberate us entirely from the tyranny of a fear "not-yet-perfected".

Finally, the destructive consequences of such "not-yet-perfected" fear with its oppression appear not only in the ethical realm but especially on the natural level of mental health—an area where psychiatry can tell its story. Here we have once again an instance in which the correlation between health and holiness becomes evident. This evidence, however, regards only the *fact* of this correlation; *how* health and holiness and even more, guilt and illness are specifically intertwined and what circumstances will activate this connection —such a description is virtually impossible. At any rate, the reason that justice, magnanimity, temperance, fear of the Lord—indeed, all virtues—are so "healthy" lies in their being in harmony with objective reality on the natural and supernatural level. Correspondence to reality is the principle of both health and goodness.

24

The Seal of Order

Aquinas says that the second meaning of temperance is "serenity of the spirit" (*quies animi*). It is obvious that this proposition does not imply a purely subjective state of mental calm or the tranquil satisfaction which is the by-product of an unassuming, leisurely life in a narrow circle. Nor does it mean a mere absence of irritation, or dispassionate equanimity. All this need not go deeper than the surface of the intellectual and spiritual life. What is meant is the serenity that fills the inmost recesses of the human being, and is the seal and fruit of order.

The Four Cardinal Virtues, pp. 147–49, translated by Daniel F. Coogan. © 1954, 1955, 1959 by Pantheon Books, Inc.; © 1965 by Harcourt Brace Jovanovich, Inc. Reprinted by permission of Harcourt Brace Jovanovich.

The purpose and goal of *temperantia* is man's inner order, from which alone this "serenity of spirit" can flow forth. "Temperance" signifies the realizing of this order within oneself.

Temperantia is distinguished from the other cardinal virtues by the fact that it refers exclusively to the active man himself. Prudence looks to all existent reality, justice to the fellow man; the man of fortitude relinquishes, in self-forgetfulness, his own possessions and his life. Temperance, on the other hand, aims at each man himself. Temperance implies that man should look to himself and his condition, that his vision and his will should be focused on himself. That notion that the primordial images of all things reside in God has been applied by Aquinas to the cardinal virtues also: the primordial divine mode of *temperantia*, he states, is the "turning of the Divine Spirit to Itself".

For man there are two modes of this turning toward the self: a selfless and a selfish one. Only the former makes for self-preservation; the latter is destructive. In modern psychology we find this thought: genuine self-preservation is the turning of man toward himself, with the essential stipulation, however, that in this movement he does not become fixed upon himself. ("Whoever fixes his eyes upon himself gives no light.") Temperance is selfless self-preservation. Intemperance is self-destruction through the selfish degradation of the powers which aim at self-preservation.

It is a commonplace though nonetheless mysterious truth that man's inner order—unlike that of the crystal, the flower, or the animal—is not a simply given and self-evident reality, but rather that the same forces from which human existence derives its being can upset that inner order to the point of destroying the spiritual and moral person. That this cleavage in human nature (provided we do not try to persuade ourselves that it does not exist) finds its explanation only in the acceptance by faith of the revealed truth of original sin, is too vast a subject to be discussed here. It seems necessary, however, to consider more closely the structure of that inner order and disorder.

Most difficult to grasp is the fact that it is indeed the essential human self that is capable of throwing itself into disorder to the point of self-destruction. For man is not really a battlefield of conflicting forces and impulses which conquer one another; and if we say that the sensuality "in us" gets the better of our reason, this is only a vague and metaphorical manner of speaking. Rather it is always our single self that is chaste or unchaste, temperate or intemperate, self-preserving or self-destructive. It is always the decisive center of the whole, indivisible person by which the inner order is upheld or upset. "It is not the good my will preserves, but the evil my will disapproves, that *I* find myself doing" (Rom 7:19).

Also, the very powers of the human being which most readily appear as the essential powers of self-preservation, self-assertion, and self-fulfillment are at the same time the first to work the opposite: the self-destruction of the moral person. In the *Summa theologica* we find the almost uncanny formulation: the powers whose ordering is the function of temperance "can most easily bring unrest to the spirit, because they belong to the *essence* of man".

25

Asceticism and Heresy

For Thomas it is plainly self-evident—indeed so self-evident that it need hardly be mentioned even to those but moderately instructed (while it may still be well not to remain silent on this point)—that the sexual powers are not a "necessary evil" but really a good. With Aristotle, he says incisively that there is something divine in human seed. It is equally self-evident to Thomas' thinking that, "like eating and drinking", the fulfillment of the natural sexual urge and its accompanying pleasure are good and not in the least sinful, assuming, of course, that order and moderation are preserved. For the intrinsic purpose of sexual power, namely, that not only now but also in days to come the children of man may dwell upon the earth and in the Kingdom of God, is not merely a good, but, as Thomas says, "a surpassing good". Indeed, complete asensuality, unfeelingly adverse to all sexual pleasure, which some would like to regard as "properly" perfect and ideal according to Christian doctrine, is described in the *Summa theologica* not only as an imperfection but actually as a moral defect (*vitium*).

At this point, a deliberate digression is called for. The progenitive purpose of sexuality is not the sole and exclusive purpose of marriage. Yet marriage is the proper fulfillment of sexual

The Four Cardinal Virtues, pp. 153–55, translated by Daniel F. Coogan. © 1954, 1955, 1959 by Pantheon Books, Inc.; © 1965 by Harcourt Brace Jovanovich, Inc. Reprinted by permission of Harcourt Brace Jovanovich.

power. Of the three goods of marriage—community of life, offspring, and sacramental blessing (*fides, proles, sacramentum*) —it is the mutually benevolent and inviolable community of life which, according to Aquinas, is the special benefit conferred on man "as man".

This affirmative position is clear to Thomas beyond any doubt because, more perhaps than any other Christian teacher, he takes seriously the fundamental thought of revelation, "Everything created by God is good", and thinks it through to its conclusion. These words were used by the Apostle Paul in order to reprimand, with the same reference to creation, those "hypocritical liars" who carry a "torch in their conscience" and "forbid men to marry and to enjoy certain foods" (Tim 4:2f.). Heresy and hyperasceticism are and always have been close neighbors. The Father of the Church, St. John Chrysostom, has expressed this with great emphasis; in a sermon he links the words of Scripture concerning "two in one flesh" to the physical union of the spouses and adds: "Why do you blush? Is it not pure? You are behaving like heretics!"

26

The "Order of Reason"

"The more necessary something is, the more the order of reason must be preserved in it." For the very reason that sexual power is so noble and necessary a good, it needs the preserving and defending order of reason.

Chastity as a virtue, therefore, is constituted in its essence by this and nothing else, namely, that it realizes the order of reason in the province of sexuality. Unchastity as a sin, on the other hand, is in its essence the transgression and violation of the rational order in the province of sexuality.

There is something uncomfortable about the straightforward use of the terms "reason" and "the order of reason" for us modern Christians. But this mistrust, for which, by the way, there is ample cause and reason, must not prevent us from a frank inquiry into what Thomas would have us understand by "reason" and "the order of reason".

Four facts have to be borne in mind if we wish to escape the danger of simply missing St. Thomas' meaning, even before taking a position ourselves. We must consider that Thomas' concept of "reason" and "the order of reason" is to be taken realistically, not idealistically; that it is free of all rationalistic restrictions; that it has none of the connotations of the *ratio* of the Enlightenment; and, finally, that it is not in the least spiritualistic.

The Four Cardinal Virtues, pp. 155–58, translated by Daniel F. Coogan. © 1954, 1955, 1959 by Pantheon Books, Inc.; © 1965 by Harcourt Brace Jovanovich, Inc. Reprinted by permission of Harcourt Brace Jovanovich.

The concept "order of reason", first of all, does not signify that something must agree with the imperative of an "absolute reason" detached from its object. *Reason* includes a reference to reality; indeed, it is itself this reference. "In accord with reason" is in this sense that which is right "in itself", that which corresponds to reality itself. The order of reason accordingly signifies that something is disposed in accordance with the truth of real things.

Secondly, *ratio* is not that reason which arbitrarily restricts itself to the province of purely natural cognition. *Ratio* here signifies—in its widest sense—man's power to grasp reality. Now, man grasps reality not only in natural cognition but also—and this reality is a higher object of knowledge and the process of grasping it a higher process—by faith in the revelation of God. If therefore the *Summa theologica* states that Christ is the chief Lord (*principalis Dominus*), the first owner of our bodies, and that one who uses his body in a manner contrary to order, injures Christ the Lord himself, Thomas is not of the opinion that this proposition exceeds the pattern of "mere" rational order, but rather that for Christian thought to be guided by divine revelation is the very highest form of "accord with reason"—this in spite of the fact that elsewhere Thomas knows how to distinguish sharply between natural and supernatural cognition. "The order of reason", accordingly, is the order which corresponds to the reality made evident to man through faith and knowledge.

Thirdly, the emphatic and ever recurrent stress on reason and the order of reason in works of Aquinas is obviously not to be understood in the sense which the Enlightenment has given to these terms. "To realize the order of reason in the province of sexuality" is a proposition which one most certainly would not want to understand as an incitement or permission to lift that which natural feeling and propriety surround and protect with the sheltering obscurity of concealment and silence into the crude and artificial light of a shallow "know-it-all" view. Rather, Thomas expressly co-ordinates modesty with chastity, whose function is to see to it that this silence and this obscurity are not destroyed either by shamelessness or uninhibited rationalizing, or spotlighted by the methods of "sexual instruction". This, therefore, forms part of the "order of reason" too.

Fourthly, the Thomistic concept of reason might be misinterpreted spiritualistically, a facile temptation to some. The proposition that "the essential and proper good of man is existence in accord with reason" could be read to mean: "Constant spiritual awareness is what distinguishes the specifically human condition; everything that clouds this awareness is unspiritual, consequently unworthy of the human condition, and therefore evil." Applied to the province here under discussion such a spiritualistic interpretation might easily lead to the following conclusion: "In the act of procreation, reason is so overwhelmed by the abundance of pleasure that, as the philosopher says, spiritual cognition becomes impossible . . . ; thus there can be no act of begetting without sin." Now this last sentence is actually to be found in the *Summa theologica* of St. Thomas—but as an "objection", that is, as an expressly confuted opinion, as a negation to which a clear affirmation is opposed. The affirmation is worded as follows: "As long as the sexual act itself corresponds to the rational order, the abundance of pleasure does not conflict with the proper mean of virtue. . . . And even the fact that reason is unable to make a free act of cognition of spiritual things simultaneously with that pleasure does not prove that the sexual act conflicts with virtue. For it is not against virtue that the workings of reason sometimes are interrupted by something that takes place in accordance with reason: otherwise it would be contrary to virtue to sleep." Do we need any further explanation in order to show how much St. Thomas's concept of reason has regard to the *whole* man—to body and soul, sensuality and spirituality? St. Thomas designates as "not in accord with reason" the opinion of some Fathers of the Church that "in Paradise the propagation of mankind would have taken place in some other manner, such as that of the angels"; indeed, St. Thomas says: The pleasure that accompanies intercourse must have been even stronger in Paradise—since mental awareness was unclouded and because of the greater delicacy of human nature and the higher sensitivity of the body. But enough of this.

27

Only the Pure of Heart
Can Perceive Beauty

That Christian doctrine does not exclude sensual enjoyment from the realm of the morally good (as against the merely "permissible") does not need to be specifically stated. But that this enjoyment should be made possible only by the virtue of temperance and moderation—that, indeed, is a surprising thought. Yet this is what we read in the *Summa theologica*, in the first question of the tractate on temperance—even if more between and behind the lines than in what is said directly. In the case of animals, it is said there, no pleasure is derived from

The Four Cardinal Virtues, pp. 166–67, translated by Daniel F. Coogan. © 1954, 1955, 1959 by Pantheon Books, Inc.; © 1965 by Harcourt Brace Jovanovich, Inc. Reprinted by permission of Harcourt Brace Jovanovich.

the activity of the other senses, such as the eye and the ear, except as they affect the satisfaction of the drives of hunger and sex; only because of the promise of food is the lion "happy" when he spies a stag or hears his call. Man, by contrast, is able to enjoy what is seen or heard for the sensual "appropriateness" alone which appeals to the eye and the ear—by this, nothing else but sensual beauty is to be understood. One frequently reads and hears that in intemperance man sinks to the level of the beast—a dictum to be used with caution, for intemperance (like temperance) is something exclusively human; neither angel nor animal can know it. But keeping this distinction in mind, the sentence becomes meaningful: unchaste lust has the tendency to relate the whole complex of the sensual world, and particularly of sensual beauty, to sexual pleasure exclusively. Therefore only a chaste sensuality can realize the specifically human faculty of perceiving sensual beauty, such as that of the human body, as beauty, and to enjoy it for its own sake, for its "sensual appropriateness", undeterred and unsullied by the self-centered will to pleasure. It has been said that only the pure of heart can laugh freely and liberatingly. It is no less true that only those who look at the world with pure eyes can experience its beauty.

28

The Fruit of Purity

Temperance is liberating and purifying. This above all: temperance effects purification.

If one approaches the difficult concept of purity through this strangely neglected gateway and begins to understand purity as the fruit of purification, the confusing and discordant sounds which usually obscure this notion and move it dangerously close to Manichaeism are silenced. From this approach the full and unrestricted concept of purity—so different from the currently accepted one—comes into view.

This is the purity meant by John Cassian when he calls purity of heart the immanent purpose of temperance: "It is served by solitude, fasting, night watches, and penitence." It is this wider concept of purity which is referred to in St. Augustine's statement that the virtue of temperance and moderation aims at preserving man uninjured and undefiled for God.

But what does this unrestricted concept of purity stand for? It stands for that crystal-clear, morning-fresh freedom from self-consciousness, for that selfless acceptance of the world which man experiences when the shock of a profound sorrow carries him to the brink of existence or when he is touched by the shadow of death. It is said in the Scriptures: "Grave illness sobers the soul" (Eccles 31:2); this sobriety belongs to the essence of purity. That most disputed statement of Aristotle:

The Four Cardinal Virtues, pp. 205–6, translated by Daniel F. Coogan. © 1954, 1955, 1959 by Pantheon Books, Inc.; © 1965 by Harcourt Brace Jovanovich, Inc. Reprinted by permission of Harcourt Brace Jovanovich.

tragedy causes purification, catharsis, points in the same direction. Even the Holy Spirit's gift of fear, which St. Thomas assigns to *temperantia*, purifies the soul by causing it to experience, through grace, the innermost peril of man. Its fruit is that purity by dint of which the selfish and furtive search for spurious fulfillment is abandoned. Purity is the perfect unfolding of the whole nature from which alone could have come the words: "Behold the handmaid of the Lord!" (Lk 1:38).

A new depth here opens to our view: purity is not only the fruit of purification; it implies at the same time readiness to accept God's purifying intervention, terrible and fatal though it might be; to accept it with the bold candor of a trustful heart, and thus to experience its fruitful and transforming power.

29

Temperance Creates Beauty

To the virtue of temperance as the preserving and defending realization of man's inner order, the gift of beauty is particularly co-ordinated. Not only is temperance beautiful in itself, it also renders men beautiful. Beauty, however, must here be understood in its original meaning: as the glow of the true and the good irradiating from every ordered state of being, and not in the patent significance of immediate sensual appeal. The

The Four Cardinal Virtues, pp. 203–4, translated by Richard and Clara Winston. © 1954, 1955, 1959 by Pantheon Books, Inc.; © 1965 by Harcourt Brace Jovanovich, Inc. Reprinted by permission of Harcourt Brace Jovanovich.

beauty of temperance has a more spiritual, more austere, more virile aspect. It is of the essence of this beauty that it does not conflict with true virility, but rather has an affinity to it. Temperance, as the wellspring and premise of fortitude, is the virtue of mature manliness.

The infantile disorder of intemperance, on the other hand, not only destroys beauty, it also makes man cowardly; intemperance more than any other thing renders man unable and unwilling to "take heart" against the wounding power of evil in the world.

It is not easy to read in a man's face whether he is just or unjust. Temperance or intemperance, however, loudly proclaim themselves in everything that manifests a personality: in the order or disorder of the features, in the attitude, the laugh, the handwriting. Temperance, as the inner order of man, can as little remain "purely interior" as the soul itself, and as all other life of the soul or mind. It is the nature of the soul to be the "form of the body".

This fundamental principle of all Christian psychology not only states the in-forming of the body by the soul, but also the reference of the soul to the body. On this, a second factor is based: temperance or intemperance of outward behavior and expression can have its strengthening or weakening repercussion on the inner order of man. It is from this point of view that all outer discipline—whether in the sphere of sexual pleasure or in that of eating and drinking, of self-assertion, of anger and of the gratification of the eye—obtains its meaning, its justification and its necessity.

30

"Concupiscence of the Eyes"

It would be easy enough to render the words *studiositas* and *curiositas*, following the dictionary, as "desire for knowledge" or "zeal", for the first, and "inquisitiveness", for the second. But this would amount to suppressing their most important meaning. Further, one might think that we speak but trivially and condescendingly of the virtue of the "good student" and of the more or less harmless weakness of the woman gossiping across the back fence.

Studiositas, curiositas—by these are meant temperateness and intemperance, respectively, in the natural striving for knowledge; temperateness and intemperance, above all, in the indulgence of the sensual perception of the manifold sensuous beauty of the world; temperateness and intemperance in the "desire for knowledge and experience", as St. Augustine puts it.

Nietzche said that wisdom "puts limits to knowledge". Whatever he himself may have meant by this, there is no doubt that the will-to-knowledge, this noble power of the human being, requires a restraining wisdom, "in order that man may not strive immoderately for the knowledge of things".

But in what consists such immoderateness? . . .

The Four Cardinal Virtues, pp. 200–202, translated by Daniel F. Coogan. © 1954, 1955, 1959 by Pantheon Books, Inc.; © 1965 by Harcourt Brace Jovanovich, Inc. Reprinted by permission of Harcourt Brace Jovanovich.

The essential intemperateness of the urge for knowledge is "concupiscence of the eyes". Only by working through a tangled thicket of vague and false interpretation, and by following the guidance of St. Augustine and St. Thomas, can we obtain a grasp of the true significance of this word of Scripture. It has, as will be seen, an immediate relevance to modern man.

There is a gratification in seeing that reverses the original meaning of vision and works disorder in man himself. The true meaning of seeing is perception of reality. But "concupiscence of the eyes" does not aim to perceive reality, but to enjoy "seeing". St. Augustine says of the "concupiscence of the palate" that it is not a question of satiating one's hunger but of tasting and relishing food; this is also true of *curiositas* and the "concupiscence of the eyes". "What this seeing strives for is not to attain knowledge and to become cognizant of the truth, but for possibilities of relinquishing oneself to the world", says Heidegger in his book *Being and Time* . . . .

Accordingly, the degeneration into *curiositas* of the natural wish to see may be much more than a harmless confusion on the surface of the human being. It may be the sign of complete rootlessness. It may mean that man has lost his capacity for living with himself; that, in flight from himself, nauseated and bored by the void of an interior life gutted by despair, he is seeking with selfish anxiety and on a thousand futile paths that which is given only to the noble stillness of a heart held ready for sacrifice and thus in possession of itself, namely, the fullness of being. Because he is not really living from the wellspring of his nature, he seeks, as Heidegger says, in "curiosity, to which nothing remains closed", the pledge of a supposedly genuine "living Life".

Not for nothing does Holy Scripture name "concupiscence of the eyes" among the three powers which constitute the world that "lieth in the power of evil" (1 Jn 2:16; 5:19).

It reaches the extremes of its destructive and eradicating power when it builds itself a world according to its own image and likeness: when it surrounds itself with the restlessness of a perpetual moving picture of meaningless shows, and with the literally deafening noise of impressions and sensations breathlessly rushing past the windows of the senses. Behind the flimsy pomp of its façade dwells absolute nothingness; it is a world of, at most, ephemeral creations, which often within less than a quarter hour become stale and discarded, like a newspaper or magazine swiftly scanned or merely perused; a world which, to the piercing eye of the healthy mind untouched by its contagion, appears like the amusement quarter of a big city in the hard brightness of a winter morning: desperately bare, disconsolate and ghostly.

The destructiveness of this disorder which originates from, and grows upon, obsessive addiction, lies in the fact that it stifles man's primitive power of perceiving reality; that it makes man incapable not only of coming to himself but also of reaching reality and truth.

If such an illusory world threatens to overgrow and smother the world of real things, then to restrain the natural wish to see takes on the character of a measure of self-protection and self-defense. *Studiositas*, in this frame of reference, primarily signifies that man should oppose this virtually inescapable seduction with all the force of selfless self-preservation; that he should hermetically close the inner room of his being against the intrusively boisterous pseudo-reality of empty shows and sounds. It is in such an asceticism of cognition alone that he may preserve or regain that which actually constitutes man's vital existence: the perception of the reality of God and his creation, and the possibility of shaping himself and the world according to this truth, which reveals itself only in silence.

The Two Sides of the Coin
That Is Truth

31

Reality and the Knowing Mind

"Reality" is everything that stands "before" our sensory and mental perception, everything that exists independent from our perceiving it. "Real" in this sense is anything that can "stand in our way". Here the original meaning of the word "object" as *ob-iectum* (thrown against) is revealed and confirmed. "Non-real" is anything that exists only in thought (whereas the thought itself is real); Scholastic philosophy named it *ens rationis*, a thing of the mind. Reality, from *realis* [real], means the quintessence of everything whose being is independent from any thought. Whenever Thomas Aquinas refers to this "reality", not looking at its superabundant variety but merely its objective nonmental character, he uses *res*—"a core term of the Latin language", according to Theodore Haecker, "a gift of the Romans to the entire world".

The correlations between the mind and objective reality are identified in three expressions: contemplating the role of the mind, we say "to know"; contemplating reality, we say "to be known"; and equally contemplating both, we speak of "truth".

> Beings endowed with the ability to know are distinct from those not so endowed inasmuch as the latter do not have any other form but their own, while the former are capable

Originally published in *Die Wirklichkeit und das Gute* (Munich: Kösel-Verlag, 1963). Translated by Lothar Krauth.

> of having also the form of the other being . . . . It is for
> this reason the Philosopher says that the human soul, in a
> certain sense, is all in all.

To *have* a form means: to be a specific being. Each thing is what it is because of the form it has.

"To know", then, means: to have the forms of other things, to be the other thing, to be identical with the other thing — to be all in all. "For this reason the Philosopher says that the soul is all in all." *Connaître, c'est devenir un autre* (To know means to become another).

A distinction must be made between knowing as dynamic process and knowing as accomplished ontological fact.

Knowing as process has an active and a passive dimension. The active side: the preter-material, intelligible core of an object's being is extracted from its sense-oriented material wrapping; a spontaneous penetration takes place into the realm of the nonmaterial essence of an object. It is through this activity that the knowing mind as such actuates and realizes itself. The passive side: the essential form of the respective reality is apprehended and received.

This active-passive process, though, is quite irrelevant in view of knowing as accomplished ontological fact, or rather: the active and passive dynamic is indeed necessary for knowing to take place, but it does not constitute the essence of knowing as such. The essence of knowing consists in *having* the forms of the objective reality; knowing as accomplished ontological fact is not an "activity" of the knowing mind but its actuality. Knowing, then, consists of the mind's "being-in-relation" to the world of objective entities. Knowing is the identity between the knowing soul and reality, viewed from the knowing soul that actuates its proper potentiality precisely in this identity.

The knowing mind's "being-in-relation" with what is real constitutes, in fact, the conceptual content of "truth". Truth is *conformitas*, "being-one-form", and *adaequatio*, "being-the-same" — both terms taken in their literal meaning — between reality and knowing. And this relation arises in the very act of knowing: "In the operation of the knowing mind the relation that is identification is completed, and in this consists the essence of truth." Truth is nothing else but the relation of identity between the mind and reality, a relation originating and accomplished in the act of knowing; reality, in this relation, is the standard for the knowing mind.

32

Incomprehensible Comprehensibility

Anything that originates with an idea in a human mind possesses by this very fact the quality of being fundamentally comprehensible. Whatever comes about by human thinking, no matter how much of a material form it has taken on (like a machine, an appliance, a sculpture), itself possesses by necessity the character of such thinking, which then can be "repeated" in the beholder's own mind. Laypeople not versed in mathematics may understand nothing, say, about the structure and function of a computer, and yet each of their possible questions, in principle, has an answer that in turn can be understood, rendering the entire subject comprehensible.

This has a perfect analogy: the natural world around us can be empirically known precisely because it has first been "thought" by the Creator. This approach alone, at any rate, opens the way for a more profound inquiry in order to make

---

"Kreatürlichkeit", originally published in *Buchstabier-Übungen* (Munich: Kösel-Verlag, 1980). Translated by Lothar Krauth.

the world's comprehensibility ultimately plausible. Moreover, this comprehensibility of objects and even of human nature as such appears to be, strictly speaking, more than just an empirical finding. We are evidently utterly incapable of so much as imagining anything that could be real and basically incomprehensible at the same time. As Charles S. Peirce states it: "We cannot even talk about anything but a knowable object. . . . The absolutely unknowable is a non-existent existence."

An academic colleague, a professor of logic, once put this critical question to me: Would the sky really cave in if we had to admit that there are realities that simply cannot be known? Have not the physicists, in fact, already been confronted with precisely such unknowable realities, for example, in their research into the physics of light? In response I asked my colleague whether the physicists had therefore abandoned for good any search for answers. He replied, "Of course not, naturally!" Well, is this not an indication of how everybody "naturally" presumes that even those realities that for now are beyond the reach of our knowledge would still be, in principle, comprehensible? Whoever thinks it makes sense to explore what has so far been unknown implicitly affirms the comprehensibility of the world. Eminent scientists, reflecting on their own domain's deeper foundations that lie beyond "science", have time and again recognized and articulated this truly amazing fact. I quote but two testimonies. It was Albert Einstein who said, "What is most incomprehensible about nature is the fact that it is comprehensible." And Louis de Broglie remarks, "We never wonder quite enough at the fact that scientific knowledge is possible at all." We should keep in mind, of course, what Gilson has added: that "the question of what makes science possible is itself, indeed, not a scientific question".

I am rather convinced that neither Einstein nor de Broglie had in mind, or had even heard about, the concept of the "truth of all things". And yet they describe the very same reality actually expressed by this concept, a concept that in former times was regarded as fundamental. The concept of the "truth of all things" means precisely what Albert Einstein and Louis de Broglie have discovered and identified: the ontological intelligibility of nature and all reality as such, which alone makes reality accessible to our searching mind.

33

The "Truth of All Things"

If you study any philosophical treatise of our present era you will with almost absolute certainty *not* encounter the concept, and much less the expression, "the truth of all things". This is no mere accident. The generally prevailing philosophical thinking of our time has no room at all for this concept; it is, as it were, "not provided for". It makes sense to speak of truth with regard to thoughts, ideas, statements, opinions—but not with regard to things. Our judgments regarding reality may be true (or false); but to label as "true" reality itself, the "things", appears to be rather meaningless, mere nonsense. Things are real, not "true"!

Looking at the historical development of this situation, we find that there is much more to it than the simple fact of a cer-

---

"Wahrheit der Dinge—ein verschollener Begriff", originally published in *Festschrift für Leo Brandt* (Köln-Opladen: Westdeutscher-Verlag, 1969). Translated by Lothar Krauth.

tain concept or expression not being used; we find not merely the "neutral" absence, as it were, of a certain way of thinking. No, the nonuse and absence of the concept, "the truth of all things", is rather the result of a long process of biased discrimination and suppression or, to use a less aggressive term: of elimination.

34

Things Can Be Known
Because They Are Created

The fundamental statement about the "truth of all things" is found in St. Thomas' *Questiones disputatae de veritate*; it reads: *res naturalis inter duos intellectus constituta (est)*; whatever is real in nature is placed between two knowing agents, namely—so the text continues—between the *intellectus divinus* [God's mind] and the *intellectus humanus* [human mind].

These "coordinates" place all reality between the absolutely creative, inventive knowledge of God and the imitating, "informed" knowledge of us humans and thus present the total realm of reality as a structure of interwoven original and reproduced conceptions.

Originally published in *Unaustrinkbares Licht* (Munich: Kösel-Verlag, 1963). Translated by Lothar Krauth.

Based on this twofold orientation of all things—so Thomas continues his reasoning—the concept of the "truth of all things" is also twofold: first, it means "thought by God"; second, it means "knowable to the human mind". The statement, "All things are true", would therefore mean, on one hand, that all things are known by God in the act of creation and, on the other hand, that all things are by their nature accessible and comprehensible to the human mind.

All things can be known by us because they spring from God's thought. Because they originated in God's mind, things have not only their specific essence in themselves and for themselves, but precisely because they originated in God's mind, things have as well an essence "for us". All things are intelligible, translucent, clear and open because they are created by God's thought, and for this reason they are essentially spirit related. The clarity and lucidity that flows from God's knowledge into things, together with their very being (more correctly: *as* their very being)—this lucidity alone makes all things knowable for the human mind. St. Thomas, in a commentary on Scripture, remarks: "A thing has exactly as much light as it has reality." And in one of his late works, in his commentary on the *Liber de causis*, we find a profound statement that expresses the same thought in almost mystical terms: *ipsa actualitas rei est quoddam lumen ipsius*; "the reality of a thing is itself its light"—and "reality" is understood here as "being created"! It is precisely this "light" that makes a thing visible to our eyes. In short: things can be known because they are created.

35

Things Are Unfathomable
Because They Are Created

We are quite capable not only of perceiving things as such but
also of perceiving the correlation between those things and
our own concept of them. This means: we are able to go beyond a mere uncritical awareness of things and to gain judi-
cious and reflective knowledge. To put it differently: not only
can human knowledge be true, it can also be knowledge of the
truth.

In the correlation between all things and the creative
"knowing" of God lies the primordial and only "truth" of
these things, a truth that in its turn makes human knowledge
at all possible: *cognitio est quidam veritatis effectus*, as St. Thomas
states, again using an expression that somehow turns our
common thinking upside down—our knowledge is the product of truth, flowing indeed from the "truth of all things"!

That correlation, I repeat, between the reality of all nature
and the prototypical creative "knowing" of God, this correlation itself can never formally be known!

We can indeed know a thing but not its formal *truth*. We
perceive a reproduction but not its correspondence to the original, not the correlation between the thought and its actualiza-
tion. This correlation that—again—primarily constitutes the
formal "truth of all things" we cannot know. Here we have

Originally published in *Unaustrinkbares Licht* (Munich: Kösel-Verlag,
1963). Translated by Lothar Krauth.

arrived at a point where it becomes evident that being true and being unfathomable go together, and that the comprehensibility of a thing can never be fully exhausted by any finite mind —for all things are created, which means that the reason they are knowable is by necessity also the reason they are unfathomable.

"All things are true"—this means primarily, then, that all things are conceived by God. We would be thoroughly misunderstanding this statement, though, if we took it as an assertion about *God* only, as a declaration only about divine action directed toward things. No so! This statement speaks about the structure of *things*. It expresses in different terms St. Augustine's notion that things exist because God sees them, whereas *we* see things because they exist. It states that the existence and essence of things *consists* in their being conceived by the *Creator*. As we have said before, "true" is an ontological designation, a synonym for "real". *Ens et verum convertuntur* [being and truth are interchangeable]; it means the same when I say, "something real", or when I say, "something conceived by God". It is essential to all existing things (insofar as they are created) to be modeled after an original idea that resides in the absolutely creative mind of God. *Creatura in Deo est creatrix essentia*, the created thing subsists in God as creative essence—so St. Thomas puts it in his commentary on St. John.

The correlation, however, between the original idea in God and its created reproduction, which formally and primarily constitutes the truth of all things, we can never directly apprehend. We can never find a viewpoint that would allow us to compare the idea with its image. We are utterly incapable of observing—as spectators, as it were—the emanation of things from God's mind. For this reason our questing mind in its search for the essence of things, even of the humblest and simplest things, finds itself perforce on a path without an attainable destination. This is so because all things are created; it is so because the inner lucidity of all things flows from their original idea in the infinitely radiant fullness of the Divine Mind.

36

Negative Philosophy, Negative Theology

We need only treat of the *philosophia negativa* of St. Thomas —even though he has stated the principles of a *theologia negativa* as well. But then this aspect is usually not at all readily visible in standard expositions; often enough it is outright ignored. Hardly ever do you find it mentioned that the treatise on God in the *Summa theologica* begins with this statement: "We cannot know what God is, only what he is *not.*" I am not aware of any textbook on Thomistic philosophy that contains St. Thomas' respective thought as expressed in his commentary on Boethius' *De Trinitate*: There exist three levels of human knowledge about God; the lowest recognizes God as active in creation; the second sees him mirrored in spiritual beings; and the highest level knows God as the One Unknown—*tamquam ignotum*! And then, indeed, this statement from the *Questiones disputatae*: "This is the ultimate human knowledge about God—to know that we do not know God"; *quod (homo) sciat se Deum nescire*.

As for the negative element in St. Thomas' *philosophy*, we have his remark about the philosophers whose inquiries have not even succeeded in grasping the essence of a single gnat, a sentence found in an exposition written in an almost casual tone on the *Symbolum Apostolicum* [Apostles' Creed]. This statement, however, stands in rather close correlation to

Originally published in *Unaustrinkbares Licht* (Munich: Kösel-Verlag, 1963). Translated by Lothar Krauth.

numerous similar statements elsewhere. Some of them are strikingly "negative", for example, this one: *rerum essentiae sunt nobis ignotae*, "the essences of things are unknown to us". Yet this formulation is not at all so unusual and exceptional as it may appear at first. We could easily add a dozen or so similar statements from the *Summa theologica*, the *Summa contra Gentes*, the commentaries on Aristotle, and the *Questiones disputatae*. All those statements declare that we are ignorant about the "fundamental essences" of things, their "substantial and essential forms", their "essential differentiations". This would be the reason, Thomas points out, that we are unable to identify a thing by its essential name and that we are constrained to name things for some superficial and accidental trait. (Thomas then frequently uses as examples those utterly contrived medieval etymologies—for instance, that *lapis* [stone] derives from *laedere pedem* [to hurt one's foot].)

Not only God himself but things as well have an "eternal name" that cannot be pronounced by any human being. This is meant to be strictly taken literally, not poetically. The Western theological tradition here fully agrees with the Chinese saying: a name that can be pronounced is not the eternal name (Lao Tzu).

37

"Experience"

The following statement sounds rather aggressive and indeed is intended to: "There is no way to gain factual knowledge except the way of experience." This sentence can be understood in a quite acceptable sense. It would be hopeless, at any rate, and not worth the effort to take the manifold results of mere mental speculation and construction, be they in form of essays or entire systems, and try to defend them as "philosophy".

On the other hand, it is a not infrequent misunderstanding to consider that statement about experience to be itself a statement from experience. This should be quite evident—if not at first sight, then at least at second sight. Whoever defends its truth, indeed, has already conceded that our basic convictions, by necessity and I suppose also by right, rest as well on realities other than experience—always including experience, of course.

But what does "experience" mean? As a preliminary answer I propose this: experience is knowledge coming from direct contact with reality. Experience, however, happens—as few would doubt any longer—not only (though primarily) through sense perception in which things literally "tickle our senses", as the first sentence of *The Critique of Pure Reason* states. We "experience" something not only at that moment when our hand touches an object or our eyes see what is visible. The whole living human body acts as an infinitely

---

Originally published in *Über das Ende der Zeit: Eine geschichtsphilosophische Meditation*, new revised edition (Munich: Kösel-Verlag, 1980). Translated by Lothar Krauth.

differentiated and sensitive receptacle of this direct contact with reality and thus forms one whole organ for possible experiences.

Here now, no doubt, we have one of the basic sources of all knowledge. Nothing of all that this organ perceives in its contact with reality—the external world or indeed the reality of our own selves—nothing of all this may be disregarded if we are to gain, through the "way of experience", a more comprehensive, more penetrating knowledge of all there is. Whitehead has stated this condition in almost passionate terms; nothing must be left out, everything plays a role: the experience of the one who is awake as well as the one who sleeps or is drunk or is gripped by fear; experiences in light as also in darkness, in pain as also in happiness; the experience of the believer and the sceptic, even normal and abnormal experience. Furthermore, he adds, these experiential findings do not at all disappear when the act of experiencing is over; they are gathered and "stored": in our great institutions; in the very behavior of people; in our language and important literary works; above all, as everybody knows, in the treasure troves of science.

There are, moreover, many different ways of experiencing. I experience in a certain way that iron is heavier than aluminum. In a different way I experience—without any "proof" or explicit verification—that I am loved or hated. In a way again entirely different I perceive the specific artistry of a poem. Nevertheless, in all these instances true experiences take place; the different weights of metals, the attitudes of friend or foe, the innermost message of a poem are conveyed to me not through information from an agent elsewhere but through direct encounter with the objects, which reveal their proper qualities themselves.

And then there are experiences that can be repeated and thus verified by others; and there are experiences that cannot be communicated in this way. The experiences of a believer, for example, cannot as a rule be imparted to a nonbeliever. It is an essential characteristic of faith to effect total identification of the believer with what is believed, to such an extent that it becomes impossible to assume, even only theoretically and hypothetically, that what is believed is untrue. For the same reason a nonbeliever is unable to reproduce the conviction, be it only as a thought experiment and "pure theory", that what is believed is true. ("Let's assume the Christians are right, and let's see how far we get with it.") Faith is not something like an observatory tower or a telescope, which can be used for experiments by everyone. Only the believer with full existential commitment is capable of perceiving the light that the truth of faith sheds on all reality.

There is, again, a kind of experience that in its substance is immediately and clearly understood and identified by the one having it; and there is another kind of experience, one that may not even be registered and recognized immediately but may remain at first in a latent state. Experiences that are recalled as true experiences are possible only the moment something else happens that fails to surprise us. For example: I could never have foreseen how those closest to me might behave in an unusual situation, but the moment I witness it in fact, I am not surprised; without having been aware of it, I expected it so—because I had already previously sensed something in those persons of their innermost character but am only now able to recognize my vague notion as a true perception, as an experience.

I insist that nothing less than all this—and perhaps even more—is included in the total body of human experience. Consequently I also accept the demand of critics that philosophy must justify itself by its foundation on experience. Such de-dogmatization and emancipation of the concept of "experience", of course, clearly establishes a challenge that, to the surprise of philosophy's positivistic critics, now turns against them.

Philosophy, on the other hand, if it is obliged to deal with so vast an experiential basis, is by this very fact all the more challenged to live up to an almost superhuman claim.

The Freedom of Philosophy
and Its Adversaries

38

"I Don't Know What Freedom Means"

Once the conviction has been lost that knowledge of the truth is what actually constitutes the mind's freedom—once this is forgotten, then perhaps it may come about that the concept of "freedom" itself will grow doubtful to our understanding, vague, even obscure; we will then simply no longer know what it means.

Thus we are dismayed to find among the very last notes of André Gide the following entry: "There are thousands who are willing to give their lives to bring about better conditions for this world—more justice, a fairer distribution of temporal goods; and I hardly dare to add: more freedom, *because I do not clearly know what this means.*"

Here a vague feeling may arise that a concept like "freedom of science" could perhaps be rooted in unexpectedly profound depths, and that the contemplation of these grounds may be necessary for anybody who sets out to defend this freedom against its radical contemporary attackers.

There is a memorable statement that spells out these grounds in touching terms, namely, the ultimate freedom of the knowing mind. The statement is memorable above all because of the man who uttered or rather wrote it, and also because of the extraordinary circumstances of its composition. The man in question is an outstanding figure in Western

"Erkenntnis und Freiheit", originally published in *Buchstabier-Übungen* (Munich: Kösel-Verlag, 1980). Translated by Lothar Krauth.

thought—he is a Roman who has been educated in Athens and then, at the court of a Germanic prince, tries to hand on the wisdom of antiquity to the coming era: Boethius. And the circumstances? A prison cell. The imprisoned Boethius, waiting for his execution, assures himself of his ultimate, indestructible freedom, stating: "The human soul, by necessity, enjoys the highest freedom when it preserves itself in the contemplation of God's mind."

39

Not at Your Service

One word on the freedom of philosophy, as distinguished from the sciences: "freedom" being understood to mean "not being at the disposal of external aims and ends". The different branches of science are "free" in this sense, provided only that they are pursued philosophically and insofar as they share the freedom of philosophy. "Knowledge is free," writes Newman, "in the truest sense, as soon as and insofar as it is philosophical." In themselves, however, the various branches of science may perfectly well be placed "at the disposal of external aims and ends", and they can always be "applied" in order to satisfy a need (which is Aquinas' definition of a servile art).

To take a concrete example. The government of a country may quite well say: "In order to carry out our five-year plan,

"The Philosophical Act", in *Leisure the Basis of Culture*, pp. 102–4, translated by Alexander Dru. © 1952 Pantheon Books, Inc., New York. Used with permission.

we need physicists trained in these particular branches of their science, men who will help to put us ahead of other countries"; or: "We need medical research students to discover a more efficient cure for the 'flu." Something of this kind may happen, and still it could not be said that there was any essential interference with the science in question. But: "At the moment we need philosophers to . . ." — well, what? There is of course only one conclusion — "to elaborate, defend and demonstrate the following ideology" — it is only possible to talk or write in such terms if philosophy is being strangled to death at the very same moment. Exactly the same thing would be true if someone in authority were to say: "At the moment, we need some poets to . . ." — well, and "to what"? And again, there is only one possible answer: to prove (as the saying goes) the pen mightier than the sword in the service of some idea dictated by the state. And that, obviously, is the death of poetry. The moment such a thing happened, poetry would cease to be poetry, and philosophy would cease to be philosophy.

But this is not to say that there is no sort of connection between the fulfillment of the "common good" and the philosophy taught in a country! Only the relationship can never be established or regulated from the point of view of the general good: when a thing contains its own end, or is an end in itself, it can never be made to serve as a means to any other end — just as no one can love someone "in order that".

40

Useless and Indispensable

It is well known that Socrates evidently had great fun in point-ing out, over and over and employing exaggerated terms, how much a philosopher is really "out of touch". He himself, so he claimed, barely knew where to find the courthouse; he did not have the faintest idea about the power plays in govern-ment; he was totally ignorant of such matters as noble and humble birth: "And worse, he does not even know that he does not know all these things", as he quotes himself in iron-ical self-deprecation. He mentions the laughter of the Thra-cian maidservant who ridiculed that stargazer, the philosopher Thales, when he fell into a cistern: such laughter is still re-served for every philosopher. But I do not need to repeat these well-known anecdotes. In fact, Socrates sees the philosopher not only as the target of ridiculing laughter; he says that he, too, knows how to laugh: when someone gives a pompous speech, for instance, or when the praise of tyrants is pro-claimed, then it would be his, the philosopher's, turn to break out in laughter, and to do this "seriously"! Still, it is ulti-mately not very important to find out who is more, or less, entitled to laugh about whom.

It seems much more important to consider the question of what practical purpose might be attributed to philosophy in the life of a people. "Philosophy"—this term, of course, as we

"Über den Philosophie-Begriff Platons", in *Tradition als Herausforderung* (Munich: Kösel-Verlag, 1963). Translated by Lothar Krauth.

should briefly mention here, does not imply a specific association of persons nor a group of experts whose social function
we want to determine. Socrates pointed out that the species of
true philosophers is not at all easily recognized, "no more easily than the gods". And his other bitter remark should be
quoted here as well: the worst slander heaped upon philosophy comes from those who call themselves philosophers. So,
our intention here is not to consider the merits of a specific institution or association but rather to determine, wherever philosophy is found, its value as such for society.

The Platonist Aristotle stated philosophy's self-under-
standing in his *Metaphysics*, in which he says that all the other
sciences are more necessary, but none is more important, than
philosophy: *necessariores omnes, nulla dignior*. The "dignity" of
philosophy, however, and its due position in society is based
on the fact that nothing else can confront us with one indispensable challenge, the challenge contained in the following
question:

After we have accomplished, with an admirable amount of
intelligence and hard work, all that is necessary, after we have
provided for the basic needs of life, produced the essential
foodstuff, protected the realm of life itself—after all this, what
is the meaning of the life itself that we have thus made possible? How do we define a truly human life?

To ask this challenging question in the midst of all our accomplishments as establish ourselves in this world, to keep
this question alive through honest and precise reasoning: this
is the fundamental task of philosophy, its specific contribution
to the common good—even though, by itself, it is unable to
provide the complete answer.

41

"Liberal Arts"

"It is entirely proper and perfectly as it should be that philosophy serves no purpose" (Heidegger). The aggressive tone that emerges here derives not only from the wording but from the thought itself. By declaring that reflection on reality as such—that is, philosophy—is a meaningful, even necessary human endeavor, while admitting its lack of practical usefulness, I have in fact already rejected the totalitarian claim of a commercialized world. With this, I have already denied that some five-year plan could ever be held up as the decisive standard; I have affirmed that there is an existential realm in which such categories as "profit", "feasibility", "usefulness", "efficiency" mean nothing, a realm that nevertheless is indispensable for a truly human existence.

What appears, at first sight, as an embarrassment, a defect, a shortcoming necessarily admitted—does this now turn out to be, on the contrary, a distinction, even a privilege rightfully claimed and affirmed?

Yes, it does! This privilege is called "freedom". Philosophy by its nature is a free endeavor, and for this reason it serves no one and nothing!

At this point we should consider one very distinct dimension of the concept of "freedom". This dimension was always implicit in the traditional Western conception of freedom, and

Originally published in *Verteidigungsrede für die Philosophie* (Munich: Kösel-Verlag, 1966). Translated by Lothar Krauth.

yet a clear understanding of it is not easy to come by. First of all, we have to eliminate the misconception of freedom as nothing more than political and civil liberties. These, of course, are closely related and cannot possibly be ignored, but they are not identical with "freedom" here. This is one of the reasons that any discussion of this issue with politicians and sociologists usually ends in discord. Noninterference by outside powers such as the government is not the primary meaning of this specific freedom; we envision rather a certain inner quality. We speak of "freedom" in the same sense as is implied in a concept that comes from antiquity, the ancient expression of the *artes liberales*, the "liberal arts". "Academic freedom" should also be mentioned here; this, too, originally meant something different from a mere instance of political freedom of speech or the students' privilege of pursuing their studies at their own discretion.

Aristotle seems to be the first to have formulated explicitly the precise nature of this kind of freedom. He deals with it in a dense and difficult section of his *Metaphysics*, in direct connection with philosophy. Indeed, philosophy *alone* would be "free" in this specific sense. In what sense, then? Analyzing Aristotle's text in his *Metaphysics*, we find to our surprise that "free" there means the same as "nonpractical"! "Practical" is everything that *serves* a purpose. Precisely this, then, does not apply to philosophical reasoning or *theoria*. Philosophy is "free" insofar as it is not geared toward some purpose outside itself. Philosophy, rather, is an endeavor containing its own meaning and requires no justification from a purpose "served".

I suspect that this, at first sight, does not sound very convincing. Above all, is this not an assertion rather than an argument? And besides, are we not playing a bit here with tautology?

Quite a few things, indeed, come into play here. Our topic is not far, as it were, from the hub of the wheel where all the spokes are already almost touching each other. Let me relate at this point an experience that brought home to me important insights. In those days it still was possible, though only half-way legal, for groups of students from the [East German] totalitarian area to visit us [in West Germany] for talks and discussions. In one such circle there was mentioned, casually, a novel that at that time enjoyed much public attention but by now is virtually forgotten. When asked, our friends from "over there" reported that this novel would not be published in their country because it contained serious historical errors about the Russian Revolution, which in reality had not by no means (for example) stifled the development of the individual. We replied that such things, after all, could be researched and determined objectively—could they not? For this, of course, a totally independent discussion would be required, not necessarily a discussion in public but at any rate without "official" interference. It was further pointed out that there had to be, after all, some free space in society where such discussion could take place unimpeded. The conversation, which had begun innocently enough, at this point suddenly brought home something quite decisive—to all participants, not only to those from "over there". More precisely, two things became strikingly evident.

First: how important it is whether or not such a "free" space exists in a political commonwealth, a space where in fact and contrary to the pretended axiom the "class struggle" is suspended, as well as the five-year plan, and all "politics" to boot, all special interests, be they collective or private. A space of exactly this sort is what is meant by the ancient term *scholé*, which designates "school" and "leisure" at the same time. It means a refuge where discussion takes place, in total independence—that is, without the interference of practical goals—on just one question: How are things, "what are the facts"?

And this, secondly, suddenly sprang fresh into focus: this free space, true, must be safeguarded and protected from the outside by political power, but the possibility, even the very constitution of its freedom derives primarily from within

—from nothing else than the irrepressible determination to search for the truth, the exclusive interest, be it only for this specific moment, to find the true facts about the matter in question.

No one would find it difficult nowadays to imagine a world whose environment is almost entirely determined by a public parlance consisting of mere "slogans". All pronouncements would be made "in order to . . ." and "for the purpose of . . ."; they say nothing, they rather intend to effect something. Yet with all this, would something else not be quite evident as well: Whoever could manage to keep a keen eye on the truth of things, though surrounded by the obstruction of proclamations, banners and slogans; whoever could manage to declare from the heart what is true and real, be it even silently and to himself (such as, "But the emperor has no clothes on")—would such a person not have preserved a free space?

Once again we need to recall the original meaning of a common and seemingly familiar term. *Theoria* and "theoretical" are words that, in the understanding of the ancients, mean precisely this: a relationship to the world, an orientation toward reality characterized entirely by the desire that this same reality may reveal itself in its true being. This, and nothing else, is the meaning of truth; nothing else but the self-revelation of reality. Thus we may state that the contemplation of reality is properly called "theoretical" whenever the aim is to discover the truth and nothing else. With this I have once again quoted, almost verbatim, Aristotle's *Metaphysics*.

Never and nowhere else, except in the living and actual *theoria* of philosophy, is there found such a radical independence with regard to every imaginable subordination under practical goals. Exactly this independence is meant when we speak of the "freedom" of philosophy.

Truth and knowledge on one side, freedom on the other, are thus interrelated in a quite specific, definite sense. Perhaps it no longer sounds so strange when the medieval definition calls "liberal arts", *artes liberales*, "only those that are oriented toward knowledge alone". In the same way, and bearing in mind such experiences and reflections, the old line about the "truth that sets us free" (Jn 8:32) shows, suddenly and unexpectedly, a rather young, original and also serious face.

42

The Self-Destruction of Philosophy

To philosophize is the purest form of *speculari*, of *theorein*, it means to look at reality purely receptively — in such a way that things are the measure and the soul is exclusively receptive. Whenever we look at being philosophically, we discourse purely "theoretically" about it, in a manner, that is to say, untouched in any way whatsoever by practical considerations, by the desire to change it; and it is in this sense that philosophy is said to be above any and every "purpose".

The realization of "theorizing", in this sense, is, however, closely connected with a prior attitude of mind. It assumes the prior existence of a certain relation to the world, a relation prior to any conscious construction and foundation. We can only be theoretical in the full sense of the word (where it means a receptive vision untouched by the smallest intention to alter things, and even a complete readiness to make the will's consent or dissent dependent upon the reality we perceive through the recognition of which we give our yea or our

"The Philosophical Act", in *Leisure the Basis of Culture*, pp. 104–7, translated by Alexander Dru. © 1952 Pantheon Books, Inc., New York. Used with permission.

nay) — we can only be "theoretical" in this undiluted sense, so long as the world is something other (and something more) than a field for human activity, its material, or even its raw material. We can only be "theoretical" in the full sense of the word if we are able to look upon the world as the creation of an absolute spirit.

There is, then, a quite definite relationship to the world that is the only soil in which "pure theory" can live. The freedom to philosophize and of philosophy itself are both bound to that assumption, to that relationship, as by the firmest of ties. Nor is it to be wondered that the collapse of that relation to reality and the weakening of that tie (by virtue of which the world is viewed as a Creation and not as material for man to act upon) should keep pace with the collapse of the theoretical character of philosophy, with the loss of its superiority to a mere function, and with the decay of philosophy itself. There is a direct link between "Knowledge is power", or Bacon's other statement, that the purpose of knowledge is to furnish man with new inventions and gadgets — and Descartes' blunt statement of his aim in the *Discourse*, of replacing theoretical philosophy, in order to become the "masters and owners of nature" — and on to Marx's well-known formula: up to the present philosophy has been concerned with interpreting the world, whereas it ought to be busy altering it.

Historically speaking, the path which leads down to the suicide of philosophy is this — once the world begins to be looked upon merely as the raw material of human activity, it is only a step to the abolition of the theoretical character of philosophy. Once the world ceases to be looked upon as created, theory in the full sense of the word becomes impossible. The loss of *theoria* means *eo ipso* the loss of the freedom of philosophy: philosophy then becomes a function within society, solely practical, and it must of course justify its existence and role among the functions of society; and finally, in spite of its name, it appears as a form of work or even of "labor". Whereas my thesis (which should by now be emerging plainly with its contours well defined), is that the essence of "philosophizing" is that it transcends the world of work. It is a thesis which comprehends the assertion of the theoretical character of philosophy and its freedom; it does not, of course, in any way deny or ignore the world of work (indeed it assumes its prior and necessary existence), but it does affirm that a real philosophy is grounded in belief, that man's real wealth consists, not in satisfying his needs, not in becoming "the master and owner of nature", but in seeing what is and the whole of what is, in seeing things not as useful or useless, serviceable or not, but simply as being. The basis of this conception of philosophy is the conviction that the greatness of man consists in his being *capax universi.*

The ultimate perfection attainable to us, in the minds of the philosophers of Greece, was this: that the order of the whole of existing things should be inscribed in our souls. And this conception was afterwards absorbed into the Christian tradition in the conception of the beatific vision: "What do they not see, who see him who sees all things?"

43

To Use and to Enjoy

There is no need at all to object to the famous Marxist demand to "transform the world". On the contrary, it is good and even necessary to transform the world, not only nature but the

---

Originally published in *Verteidigungsrede für die Philosophie* (Munich: Kösel-Verlag, 1966). Translated by Lothar Krauth.

human condition as well. Yet it already becomes evident at this point that it is no less good and necessary to know the world and "interpret" it, in a purely theoretical manner, which means being guided by the desire for truth and nothing else.

It is moreover quite impossible and hopeless to transform the world in any meaningful way without having first perceived what the world is basically all about. That specific dimension of the world, of course, which absorbs the philosopher's interest remains in principle outside any conceivable scheme to transform the world, remains beyond all utilization and exploitation.

St. Augustine has emphasized the distinction between *uti* = to use, and *frui* = to enjoy, and especially between those things that we use and other things that we enjoy yet cannot and must not use. To enjoy a thing means: to accept it for and by itself and to find joy in it. To use a thing, on the other hand, says: "to make something the means to obtain what we enjoy". Perhaps we could say that philosophical contemplation is concerned with those things "that we enjoy". But this way of putting it can easily be misunderstood. It becomes clearer only if we add one other thought.

The Romans translated the Greek word *theoria* with the Latin word *contemplatio*. In the Latin translation of Aristotle's main work as well, the *Metaphysics*, used by Thomas Aquinas for his commentary, we read: *theoria id est contemplatio*. As soon as the concept of "contemplation" appears in this context, there has come to the fore—unexpectedly—another aspect that so far has been hidden but now can be identified. It was doubtless part of the ancient Platonic-Aristotelian conception of *theoria* and now completes as well our own idea of what it means, and what it might imply, to philosophize. The philosophical *theoria*, at least in its fullest expression, may in its actual occurrence indeed be almost indistinguishable from "contemplation" as conceived by the later era, the Christian West. I personally am convinced of this.

Now, however, "contemplation" means a *loving* gaze, the beholding of the beloved. We have to raise the question, then, whether philosophical reflection on reality as such may not equally presume or imply some kind of acceptance of this same reality. I hesitate to use the word "love", because it is too big. "Acceptance", on the other hand, seems too imprecise and too weak. Even those who are simply incapable of any philosophical *theoria* because they consider the objects of the world, and perhaps even human beings (excepting themselves), as so much raw material that may be useful for some purpose—even those "masters and owners of nature" could be said in a certain sense to accept reality and find it good: good, of course, for them and their aims. For the true philosopher, however, the challenge seems to be this: to acknowledge, before any consideration of specifics and without regard to usefulness, that reality *is good in itself*—all things, the world, "being" as such; yes, all that exists, and existence itself. Do we not call "desire" (*amor concupiscentiae*) our accepting attitude toward those things that are "good for us and our purposes"? And does not the acceptance of that alone which we deem "good in itself" properly deserve the name of "love"? If we consider now the precise meaning of that ancient and for us moderns somewhat enigmatic expression, "all that is, is good", *omne ens est bonum*, we find that it does not say anything substantial if not this: the world, as Creation, is willed by God, which means that it is created *in love* and is therefore, by its mere existence, good.

That we use the term "love" here is, of course, not decisive (even though, on the other hand, we should not call a primordial reality simply a "term"). What is decisive, though, is our intention to identify a precondition, not readily evident, of all philosophical *theoria*. This qualification may be more successful, indeed, if we use a negative formulation and put the following question before us: Is not philosophy, as human endeavor, equally threatened by the totalitarian demands of the marketplace *and* by the nihilistic dogma that the world as such is absurd, that any kind of being deserves to perish? And should the possibility not be recognized that both these threats may be linked by some hidden connection?

44

The Purpose of Politics

All practical activity, from practice of the ethical virtues to gaining the means of livelihood, serves something other than itself. And this other thing is not practical activity. It is having what is sought after, while we rest content in the results of our active efforts. Precisely that is the meaning of the old adage that the *vita activa* is fulfilled in the *vita contemplativa*. To be sure, the active life contains a felicity of its own; it lies, says Thomas, principally in the practice of prudence, in the perfect art of the conduct of life. But ultimate repose cannot be found in this kind of felicity. *Vita activa est dispositio ad contemplativam*; the ultimate meaning of the active life is to make possible the happiness of contemplation.

In the commentary Thomas wrote on Aristotle's *Nicomachean Ethics* there is a sentence which expresses this idea in so challenging a fashion that I hesitate to cite it here. Thomas is speaking of politics, which is the summation of all man's active cares about securing his existence. The sentence sounds almost utopian. But it is based upon a wholly illusion-free

Happiness and Contemplation, pp. 93–96, translated by Richard and Clara Winston. © 1958 Pantheon Books, Inc., New York. Used with permission.

estimate of what is commonly called "political life"; it contains the insight that politics must inevitably become empty agitation if it does not aim at something which is not political. "The whole of political life seems to be ordered with a view to attaining the happiness of contemplation. For peace, which is established and preserved by virtue of political activity, places man in a position to devote himself to contemplation of the truth." Such is the magnificent simplicity and keenness of this dictum that we scarcely dare lean on it. Yet it is nothing but an extension of the idea that contemplation is "the goal of man's whole life".

We do not mean by this to scorn or decry practical life. On the contrary, we may well say that here is the clue to the salvation and redemption of ordinary life. And here it seems proper to put in a word about the nature of hierarchical thinking. The hierarchical point of view admits no doubt about difference in levels and their location; but it also never despises lower levels in the hierarchy. Thus the inherent dignity of practice (as opposed to *theoria*) is in no way denied. It is taken for granted that practice is not only meaningful but indispensable; that it rightly fills out man's weekday life; that without it a truly human existence is inconceivable. Without it, indeed, the *vita contemplativa* is unthinkable.

But practice does become meaningless the moment it sees itself as an end in itself. For this means converting what is by nature a servant into a master—with the inevitable result that it no longer serves any useful purpose. The absurdity and the profound dangers of this procedure cannot, in the long run, remain hidden. André Gide writes in his *Journals:* "The truth is that as soon as we are no longer obliged to earn our living, we no longer know what to do with our life and recklessly squander it." Here, with his usual acuteness, Gide has described the deadly emptiness and the endless ennui which bounds the realm of the exclusively practical like a belt of lunar landscape. This is the desert which results from destruction of the *vita contemplativa*. In the light of such a recognition we suddenly see new and forceful validity in the old principle: "It is requisite for the good of the human community that there should be persons who devote themselves to the life of contemplation." For it is contemplation which preserves in the midst of human society the truth which is at one and the same time useless and the yardstick of every possible use; so it is also contemplation which keeps the true end in sight, gives meaning to every practical act of life.

45

The Defense of Freedom

There is more to Plato's thought than the fact that he opposed the Sophists. His commitment to this opposition derived its intensity from a prior affirmation. Thus the unremitting vehemence of his rejection of Sophistry is comprehensible only if we reflect on the importance which Plato attached to that good which he believed to be compromised and threatened by the Sophists.

To understand his reaction to the Sophists, we must discuss Plato's ultimate view of the meaning of intellectual or rational existence as a whole. I believe that certain elements of this view can be expressed in three concise propositions.

Proposition One: "The good of man", and a meaningful human existence, consists, as far as possible, in seeing things as they are, and in living and acting in accordance with the truth

Problems of Modern Faith, pp. 252–56, translated by Jan van Heurck. © 1985 Franciscan Herald Press, Chicago. Reprinted with permission.

thus apprehended. *Proposition Two:* Thus man's chief nourishment is truth. This does not apply only to the man of knowledge, the philosopher, the scientist. *Anyone* who wishes to live a truly human life must feed on truth. Society too lives on the public availability, the public manifestation of truth. The more the depth and breadth of the real world is revealed and made accessible, the richer existence becomes. *Proposition Three:* The natural habitat of truth is human conversation. Truth is enacted in dialogue, in discussion, in discourse: in other words, in language and the word. Thus the order of existence, including societal existence, is essentially based on the order of language, and is shaped by whether or not language is "in order". Of course, the "order" of language does not primarily involve its formal perfection. (Thus, eager as one might be to concur with Karl Kraus' famous dictum, the order of language does not, I fear, depend on the proper placement of a comma.) Instead, what is meant by the order of language is the articulation of *reality* in as undistorted and uncurtailed a form as possible.

As it happens, these same three principles constitute the foundation of that community for teaching and learning which Plato founded in Athens beside the grove of the patron daimon Akademos, in other words the Academy. But as soon as one mentions the word "Academy", one has, of course, ceased to speak of Plato alone, in that the Academy, whether rightly or wrongly, represents the paradigm from which everything "academic", from that day to this, has derived its name. For despite the obvious fact that our universities and other institutions of advanced learning differ greatly from the original Academy of ancient Greece, the concept "academic" has nevertheless retained a common or identical feature over the course of time, a feature which, moreover, it is easy to define. This feature is the fact that a "zone of truth" is deliberately set aside in the midst of society, a hedged-in space to house the autonomous engagement with reality, in which people can inquire into, discuss, and assert the truth of things without let or hindrance; a domain expressly shielded from any conceivable attempts to use it as a means to achieve certain ends, and in which all concerns irrelevant to its true purpose, whether collective or personal, whether of political, economic or ideological import, must keep silent. We have all seen dramatic proof of what it can mean to a nation to possess such a sanctuary—or not to possess it. The fact that this sanctuary represents the realization of a certain measure of freedom —not the totality of freedom, but an indispensable piece of it which is vitally necessary to man; and the fact that, although man finds external strictures and confinement intolerable, he is a being whose existence unfolds primarily on an intellectual plane, and thus suffers even more when he is not allowed to speak and communicate, i.e., to express *publicly,* what, in his own best judgment, is the true nature of things—all this is, I believe, so obvious, that it hardly bears mentioning.

In order to exist, this domain of freedom requires guarantees from outside: guarantees, that is, on the part of the political authorities, who thereby place certain limitations on their own power. But the freedom of this domain must also be established and *defended* from within—defended against that very threat, of which we have spoken, which arises not from "outside", but, to our dismay, from "inside", as an infection of intellectual life itself. I believe that the real function of the university, understood as, in the strict sense, an academic institution—that service which it performs for the "common good" and which could be performed by nothing and no one else—lies above all in evoking, promoting and fostering, through the spirit of the institution itself, that total openness or candor whose only purpose is to ensure that the whole of reality—which of course can never be wholly fathomed—is not only *disclosed* without any sham or deception, but also *articulated,* stated, in the course of that interminable debate, transcending all individual disciplines and excluding no partner and no train of reasoning, which constitutes the actual life of the university. Moreover, "academic" means, in effect, "anti-sophistical", and thus to be academic means, at the same time, to resist everything which impugns or destroys the absolute candor of the word in its expression of the bond with reality and in its character as communication. For example, to be academic means to oppose bias and oversimplification, ideological fervor, all forms of blind emotionalism. But it also implies opposition to the seduction of that which is merely well said, to the emphasis on form without substance, to arbitrary terminology, i.e., terminology which rejects dialogue, to the "put-down" as a stylistic device (the wittier it is, the worse it becomes), to language designed to smooth troubled waters by glossing over the facts, as well as to the language of revolt, to conformity held as a basic principle, and likewise to nonconformity held as a basic principle and so on.

Clearly these prerequisites of the academic life tend to lead people in different directions, and cannot easily be "lumped together" and translated into specific "measures" or policies. If the threat is intangible, the resistance to the threat cannot, by the very nature of the case, be an organized one. Nevertheless, the academic community represents a political reality of the utmost importance. For our institution of higher learning should, as a model and norm, realize the foundation on which a political life is based: the untrammelled human communication with regard for the reality, the reality of the world and of ourselves.

46

The "Intellectual" and the Church

Recently I was invited to participate in a public debate on the subject of "intellectuals and the Church". At the time I wondered whether I myself could be considered a member of that group which we were supposed to discuss. Would other people describe me as an "intellectual"? And would I be willing to accept this designation? My answer to both questions is: Probably not! But whom *do* we have in mind when we speak of the "intellectual"? And more specifically, what do we mean by this word as it is used in modern *German,* as opposed to French or English, in which it appears to have a somewhat different meaning? Naturally the term intellectual refers to someone who has attained a certain degree of knowledge, of education, of critical awareness. But this is not the distinguishing mark of the intellectual, for a person can be an outstanding scientist and yet not be classified as an intellectual. One becomes an intellectual only by virtue of a certain attitude toward the "status quo", "the Establishment" or "the system", the existing order. Thus phrases like "The Intellectual and the Church" are highly typical. We might just as easily say, "The Intellectual and the State", ". . . and the Family", ". . . and the University". If we examine the "and" more closely, we find that it implies the attitude of critical detachment, the principle of reserving one's judgment, the intention not to identify oneself with, and not to sanction, the phenomenon in question. Moreover, at the same time it implies at least the

Problems of Modern Faith, pp. 257–64, translated by Jan van Heurck. © 1985 Franciscan Herald Press, Chicago. Reprinted with permission.

propensity to the public expression or promulgation of one's views.

For example, in relation to the university, who is an "intellectual"? Whom do we really have in mind when we use this word? Certainly a German would not apply the term to the "ordinary professor" who has a "steady job" at a university, especially if he happens to be the dean of a faculty or a rector. On the other hand, in relation to the Church a professor, even a professor of theology, might very well be designated an "intellectual", although of course he would lose all claim to this title the moment, let us say, that he was appointed a bishop. Clearly, in such a case no change whatever would have occurred in his intellectual competence to form judgments. The change would have been in his relationship to the institution [in this case the Church]. At least initially, anyone employed by an institution is assumed to identify with it. If a renowned journalist becomes the official spokesman of the government, he automatically ceases to qualify as an "intellectual". As an author who wrote on theological subjects, Jean Daniélou was an "intellectual"; but clearly intellectuals ceased to accept Daniélou as one of their own as soon as he became a cardinal.

Thus one element in the concept of the (German) intellectual is the fact that he is an "outsider", that he does not belong, that he does not wish to be identified with certain phenomena. A *second* element of this concept might be that of *engagement* or "commitment". This vogue word does not simply imply that a person "stands for", or places himself in the service of, a certain cause. What it really implies is that he takes sides *against* something. It implies the will to change the status quo, to call the existing order into question. No matter how credibly or sincerely the journalist who has become a government spokesman assures his fellow journalists that he *is* in fact "committed" to his new function, he does so in vain. For this kind of commitment does *not* qualify one as an intellectual.

If this is an accurate characterization of the (German) intellectual—in other words, if he is defined primarily by his main-

tenance of a critical detachment with regard to the existing order, by his emphatic nonconformity to social institutions
—then clearly he cannot be judged in "absolute" terms. In
other words, he cannot be judged in isolation from the institution which is the object of his critique. Is the institution in
question a despotic regime founded on manifestly unjust
laws? Or is it a commonwealth whose empirical flaws result
not from the fundamental injustice of its laws, but rather from
the inadequate realization or implementation of those laws?
Or is the institution under fire the *Church?* In the latter case,
we would have to draw a further distinction: Does the intellectual critic regard himself as a Christian, or more precisely,
as a member of the Church? And of course the same question
must be asked concerning the man who *evaluates* his critique.

Clearly the intellectual is standing on solid ground when his
refusal to identify with an institution takes the form of opposition to a manifestly unjust government. This is truly his
hour of glory, and perhaps it is the only hour in which his "adversary" position is wholly justified. Suddenly he stands in a
united front with other witnesses to the truth who may be
anything but "intellectuals". Thus it becomes possible for a
journalist like Carl von Ossietzky, with his *a priori* determination to maintain a critical reserve, to end up on the same side
as a man like Bishop von Galen, who initially trusted and
promised to cooperate with the Nazis, and who only began to
protest against them *a posteriori,* on empirical grounds, i.e., on
the grounds of what he had experienced and witnessed. To be
sure, the intellectual's "hour of glory" is at the same time an
hour of trial and probation, of persecution, loss of reputation,
emigration, and perhaps even of martyrdom. And for this reason it is also the hour of the few, not of the many. For when
push comes to shove, it is revealed that, despite the fact that
we frequently speak of "intellectuals" in the plural, the intellectual is essentially an *individual* who does not, as a rule, engage in mass protest actions and who may, at most, join
forces, when occasion warrants, with a small circle of other
individualists.

Of course in the average case the intellectual cannot lay claim to that glory which is, justly, the prerogative of the heroic exception. For in the average case, the institution attacked by the intellectual, although it may be in many ways imperfect, is not fundamentally unjust. And although it is perfectly true that whenever conditions fall short of the ideal, it is not only meaningful but essential that they be subjected to public censure; nevertheless, in the average case the maintenance of a critical detachment *as a matter of general principle* is a highly problematical phenomenon.

And the problematical nature of the phenomenon is infinitely increased when the institution under fire is not "society", the parliamentary system of government, or the university, but the Church.

The first crucial issue is that of *credentials.* How does one qualify for the role of a critic? "Intellectual": the word implies insight, erudition, knowledge. What degree of special expertise must one possess in order to qualify as an "intellectual"? If a high-school student serves as editor of a school newspaper, does this mean that he is already an intellectual? Above all, where does one draw the line between the intellectual and the sophist? In the course of Plato's lifelong debate with the sophists of his time, he repeatedly utters, through the mouth of Socrates, an indictment whose relevance to contemporary life is instantly apparent: "You believe you need concern yourselves with things (facts) only to such a degree that you can talk about them in an impressive way!"

But what happens when we are dealing with the "things" or "facts" which determine and constitute the life of the Church: the Incarnation, revelation, the priesthood, the sacraments? In this case, who possesses "special expertise"? And on what grounds can he be said to possess it? "Critical detachment" might well *disqualify,* rather than qualify him for the post! In any case I believe that it should give us pause that the

New Testament mentions two groups of people who have an especially hard time understanding the essential "facts of life": the "wise", from whom the truth is actually "hidden" [cf., for example, 1 Cor 1ff.], and the wealthy—which, irritating as the fact may be, probably refers to members of the "Establishment".

This brings us to the second issue: If, generally speaking, the social critic, the "outsider", runs the risk of shutting himself out from the life of the community in which he was intended to participate; and if it is in fact true that those who insist on maintaining a "critical" posture miss out on the best things that life has to offer (Goethe never wearies of pointing out this fact: "Pleasure, joy, the participation in things is the only reality and generates reality in turn; all else is vanity and leads to nothing but disappointment")—then does not the risk become fatal when the good things of life in question are those things entrusted to the Church, of which no one can partake unless he accepts them with faith and love; unless, that is, he "belongs" without reservation? How can I truly be a member of this mystical community, and at the same time insist on maintaining a critical detachment, on being a nonconformist, on preserving my independence, and so on? Of course I do not mean to imply that there are not a great many things about the Church, in its historical and institutional manifestation, which we are *compelled* to criticize and oppose if we are to preserve its authentic life. However—and here we come to the third issue—it is quite another matter to decide whether the critical will to bring about change, which in other cases can legitimately be effected by means of revolutionary pressure, by debate and by voting on important issues, should not, in the case of the Church, operate in accordance with a different, perhaps a unique, set of rules.

One thing which suggests that change in the Church should be effected in accordance with special rules is the history of the Church itself. This history indicates that the truly successful innovators have been the *saints,* in other words human beings in whom the passionate critique of existing conditions was combined with a totally selfless integration into the institutional hierarchy of the Church. This is as true of Francis of Assissi and Ignatius of Loyola as it is of Charles de Foucauld and Pope John XXIII. During the period of the First Vatican Council, one of the most outspoken opponents of the enunciation of the dogma of papal infallibility, John Henry Newman, repeatedly expressed — and acted on — his conviction that unless one is prepared to obey the Church, all criticism of it will necessarily remain sterile. Frequently, Newman says, the demonic power of untruth has been loosed on the world when someone, defying the authority of the Church, has attempted to promote a certain truth *at the wrong time.* This same kind of spirituality, characterized by the willingness to set aside one's personal will, was manifested by Teilhard de Chardin, who for years was regarded with suspicion by other churchmen and suffered from the many obstacles they placed in the path of his work. It is this spirituality which his friend and biographer praises when he declares that Teilhard displayed a "total absence of rebellion" *(absence complète de révolte).*

Obviously the foregoing reflections do not supply us with any permanently valid guidelines as to what are the proper norms of conduct when dealing with the Church. However, I believe that one thing emerges clearly: By the very nature of the case, the intellectual who engages in criticism of the Church must obey "different" presuppositions and take different factors into account than he does in relation to other institutions.

In conclusion, I would like to sketch a sort of personal utopia, an outline of what I would like to see happen in the future. For I wonder whether, in his relationship to the Church, the contemporary intellectual has not been offered a unique opportunity to employ and to give free play to all his potentialities, his special propensities, and liberties and even his weaknesses?

For example, could not the intellectual manifest his nonconformity by expressing his disagreement with those criticisms
of the Church which are now being shouted from every roof-
top [and which thus have come to represent the "Establishment" view]? By the way, the source of the word "nonconformity" is Scripture: *nolite conformari huic saeculo,* "And be
not conformed to this world" (Rom 12:2)! Or, what about the
pleasure the intellectual might derive from the risk of really
"going it alone", i.e., taking a truly unpopular stand? It does
not take a grain of courage to attack the Pope. But how would
it be, for a change, if an intellectual chose to publicly defend,
with imagination and verbal skill, the thesis that purity is integral to the proper functioning of a human being?

There is also a place for the intellectual to manifest an aggressive irony designed to unmask, to reveal the truth. How
splendid it would be to hear someone today say something on
the order of G. K. Chesterton's remark, or rather question, as
to whether the indissolubility of marriage was not, at bottom,
a device designed to confer on the average person the reputation for being a man of his word!

But above all, has there ever existed such a challenging opportunity for the intellectual to exercise his noblest office,
truly his *nobile officium,* as this: To take up the lance of the pro-
vocative word and to fight to defend her who is despised by
all the world—namely the Church?

But as I have said, for the present, more's the pity, these notions remain nothing but a utopian dream!

Free Space in the World of Work

47

Leisure and Its Threefold Opposition

Whoever advocates leisure nowadays may already be on the defensive. We have to face an opposition that at first seems to prevail. Things are not made easier by the fact that this opposition does not come from "someone else" but indeed springs from a conflict within ourselves. Worse yet, when put on the spot, we are not even able to define exactly what we are trying to defend. For example, when Aristotle says, "We work so we can have leisure", we must admit in all honesty that we do not know what this offensive statement means.

This, I think, is our situation.

The first question, therefore, is: What is leisure? How is this concept defined in our great philosophical tradition?

I deem it advisable to attempt an answer in such a way as to deal first with those opposing forces that could be labeled "overvaluation of work". This is admittedly a tentative expression. For "work" can mean several things, at least three. "Work" can mean "activity as such". Second, "work" can mean "exertion, effort, drudgery". And third is the usage of "work" for all "useful activity", especially in the sense "useful for society". Which of the three concepts do I have in mind when I speak of the "overvaluation of work"? I would say: all three! We encounter overvaluation of activity for its own sake, as well as overvaluation of exertion and drudgery, and

"Musse und menschliche Existenz", originally published in *Tradition als Herausforderung* (Munich: Kösel-Verlag, 1963). Translated by Lothar Krauth.

—last but not least—overvaluation of the social function of work. This specifically is the three-faced demon everyone has to deal with when setting out to defend leisure.

Overvaluation of activity for its own sake. By this I mean the inability to let something simply happen; the inability to accept a kindness graciously, to be on the receiving end in general. This is the attitude of "absolute activity" that, according to Goethe, always ends bankrupt. The most extreme expression so far of this heresy can be found in a statement by Adolf Hitler: "Any activity is meaningful, even a criminal activity; all passivity, in contrast, is meaningless." This, of course, is an insane formulation, simply absurd. But "milder" forms of such insanity, I surmise, are typical of our contemporary world.

Overvaluation of exertion and drudgery. Strangely enough, this too can be found. Yes, we may even assert that the average ethical understanding of "decent" modern people is to a large extent colored by such an overvaluation of drudgery: goodness is by nature difficult, and whatever is gained without effort cannot have moral value. [The German poet] Friedrich Schiller has ridiculed this attitude in a ditty aimed at Kant:

> *Readily do I help all my friends—*
> *Too bad, I do so with pleasure;*
> *Much am I grieved that I, with this,*
> *Can gain no virtuous treasure.*

The ancients—who are for me the great Greeks Plato and Aristotle but also the famous teachers of Western Christianity —did not hold that goodness is difficult by nature and therefore will always and necessarily be so. They were well aware of the fact that the highest forms of applied goodness are indeed always effortless because they essentially flow from love. In this same way the highest forms of perception—the sudden flash of ingenious insight or true contemplation—do not really require mental labor but come without effort because they are by nature gifts. "Gifts"—this may well be the key concept. If

we consider the strange propensity toward hardship that is en-
graved into the face of our contemporaries as a distinct expectation of suffering (a more typical trait, I believe, than the oft-
deplored craving for pleasure)—if we consider this, then to
our surprise we may face the question: Could perhaps the
deepest reason be the people's refusal to accept a gift, no matter
where it comes from?

Overvaluation of the social function of work. Not much has to
be said to show how this trait dominates contemporary soci-
eties. We should, however, think not just of those totalitarian
"five-year plans" whose infamy lies not so much in their attempt to order everything as rather in their claim to provide
the exclusive value standards for all aspects of life, not only industrial production but the personal life of individuals as well.
Oh yes, the nontotalitarian world, too, can effectively be dominated by the dictatorship of "social usefulness".

At this point we should recall the ancient distinction between *artes liberales* and *artes serviles,* between "free" and
"servile" activities. This distinction states that some human
activities contain their purpose in themselves and other activities are ordered toward a purpose outside themselves and thus
are merely "useful". This idea may at first appear rather out-
moded and pedantic. And yet it deals with something of contemporary political relevance. The question, "Are there
'free' activities?", translated into the jargon of totalitarian so-
cieties would ask: "Are there human activities that in themselves neither require nor accept any justification based on the
provisions of a five-year plan?" The ancients have answered
this question with a decisive "yes". The answer in a totalitarian environment would be an equally decisive: "No! Humans
are defined by their function. Any 'free' activity that does not
serve a socially useful purpose is undesirable and should therefore be liquidated."

If we now direct our attention from the threefold overvaluation of work toward the concept of "leisure", then one
thing becomes immediately clear: there is no room for it in

such a world. The idea of leisure here is not only preposterous but morally suspect. As a matter of fact, it is absolutely incompatible with the prevailing attitude. The idea of leisure is diametrically opposed to the totalitarian concept of the "worker", and this under each of the three aspects of work we have considered.

Against the idolizing of "activity". Leisure is essentially "nonactivity"; it is a form of silence. Leisure amounts to that precise way of being silent which is a prerequisite for listening in order to hear; for only the listener is able to hear. Leisure implies an attitude of total receptivity toward, and willing immersion in, reality; an openness of the soul, through which alone may come about those great and blessed insights that no amount of "mental labor" can ever achieve.

Against the overvaluation of drudgery. Leisure means an attitude of celebration. And celebration is the opposite of exertion. Those who are basically suspicious of achievement without effort are by the same token as unable to enjoy leisure as they are unable to celebrate a feast. To truly celebrate, however, something else is required; more on this shortly.

Against the overvaluation of social usefulness. Leisure implies that a person is freed for this period of time from any social function. Yet leisure does not mean the same as a "break". A break, whether for an hour or three weeks, is designed to provide a respite from work in anticipation of more work; it finds its justification in relation to work. Leisure is something entirely different. The essence of leisure is not to assure that we may function smoothly but rather to assure that we, embedded in our social function, are enabled to remain fully human. That we may not lose the ability to look beyond the limits of our social and functional station, to contemplate and celebrate the world as such, to become and be that person who is essentially oriented toward the whole of reality. And that all this be achieved through our own free disposition, which contains its own significance and is not "geared toward" anything.

True culture does not flourish except in the soil of leisure —provided we mean by "culture" whatever goes beyond the mere necessities of life yet is nonetheless indispensable for the fullness of human existence. If culture is thus rooted in leisure, where, then, does leisure find its roots? How can we be enabled to "achieve leisure" (as the classical Greeks put it)? What can be done to prevent our becoming mere "workers" who are totally absorbed trying to function properly? I have to admit that I am unable to give a specific and practical answer to this question. The basic difficulty is such that it cannot be remedied with a simple decision, be it ever so well intentioned. Still, we can point out why this is so.

It is well known that physicians for some time now have reminded us how important it is for our health to have leisure —and they are certainly correct. But: it is impossible to "achieve leisure" in order to stay or to become healthy, not even in order to "save our culture"! Some things can be approached only if they are seen as meaningful in and by themselves. They cannot be accomplished "in order to" effect something else. (Thus it is impossible, for example, to love someone "in order to . . ." and "for the purpose of . . ."). The order of certain realities cannot be reversed; to try it anyway is not only inappropriate but simply doomed to failure.

Related to our question, this means: if leisure is not conceived as meaningful in and by itself, then it is plainly impossible to achieve. Here we should once again mention the celebration of a feast. Such a celebration combines all three elements that also constitute leisure: first, nonactivity and repose; second, ease and absence of exertion; third, leave from the everyday functions and work. Everybody knows how difficult an endeavor it is for us moderns really to celebrate. Indeed, this difficulty is identical with our inability to achieve leisure. The reason that our celebrations fail is the same reason that we fail to achieve leisure.

At this point there appears an inevitable consideration that to most people, as I have frequently experienced, seems quite uncomfortable. Put in a nutshell, it is this: to celebrate means to proclaim, in a setting different from the ordinary everyday, our approval of the world as such. Those who do not consider reality as fundamentally "good" and "in the right order" are not able to truly celebrate, no more than they are able to "achieve leisure". In other words: leisure depends on the precondition that we find the world and our own selves agreeable. And here follows the offensive but inevitable consequence: the highest conceivable form of approving of the world as such is found in the worship of God, in the praise of the Creator, in the liturgy. With this we have finally identified the deepest root of leisure.

We should expect, I believe, that humanity will make strenuous efforts to escape the consequences of this insight. It may try, for example, to establish "artificial" feast days in order to avoid the ultimate and true approval of reality—while producing a resemblance of genuine celebration through the immense display of outward arrangements supported by the political authorities. In reality, the "organized" recreation of such pseudocelebrations is merely a more hectic form of work.

It would be a misconception to assume that this proposition regarding the cultic essence of all celebration and the cultic roots of leisure and culture would be a specifically Christian thesis. What in our days is called "secularism" represents perhaps not so much the loss of a Christian outlook as rather the loss of some more fundamental insights that have traditionally constituted humanity's patrimony of natural wisdom. I believe that our thesis on leisure and culture is part of this patrimony. It was the Greek Plato, long before Christianity, who in his old age formulated this thesis by employing the imagery of a magnificent myth. Plato asks whether there would be no respite for the human race, destined as it seems for labor and suffering. And he replies, Yes indeed, there is a respite: "The gods, out of compassion for us humans who are born into hardship, provided respite by granting periodic cultic celebrations, and by giving us, to join in our feasts, the Muses with their leaders Apollo and Dionysus, so that we may be sustained by joyfully conversing with the gods, and be lifted up and given a sense of direction." And the other great Greek,

Aristotle, of a more critical turn of mind than his teacher Plato and, as is well known, less given to images from myth—even Aristotle has expressed the same insight in his usual dispassionate manner. In the same *Nichomachean Ethics* that also contains the sentence quoted at the beginning ("We work so we can have leisure") we read that we cannot achieve leisure insofar as our human nature is concerned but only insofar as we possess the divine spark in us.

48

Earthly Contemplation

The great thinkers of the Western tradition regard as a self-evident and inviolable truth the idea that the ultimate satiation of our desires awaits us only on the other side of death, and that this beatitude will take the form of *seeing*. However, this eschatological assertion concerning the perfection which ultimately lies in store for us has always, at the same time, been interpreted as a commentary on the earthly existence of man in this world. It has in fact been interpreted to mean: not only in the life to come, but also in his material existence in history, man is, to the very roots of his being, a creature designed for and desiring vision; and this is true to such a degree that the extent of a man's happiness is only as great as his capacity for contemplation.

Problems of Modern Faith, pp. 149–54, translated by Jan van Heurck. © 1985 Franciscan Herald Press, Chicago. Reprinted with permission.

At first glance this notion appears so remote from the contemporary view of man as to border on the absurd. This apparent absurdity is the subject of my discourse. The concept of contemplation which I have just outlined implies and presupposes several things which are not immediately apparent. For example, in the first place it implies that man in this world is capable of visionary knowledge, that his means of ascertaining the nature of reality are not exclusively mental, i.e., do not consist solely of working with concepts and of intellectual exertion. It implies and presupposes the celebration of the simple act of looking at things. Anyone who disputes the possibility of such a celebration cannot accept the thesis of the joy of contemplation. However, clearly the denial of this joy can have a far-reaching effect on our everyday lives and can even extend its influence into the political sphere. For example, the inhumanity of life in a totalitarian state which places all its emphasis on man in his aspect as a *worker* derives, in part, from the fact that even in his intellectual and spiritual existence, man is defined as a laborer who, although he experiences pauses in his work, does not experience *rest*.

Our theory of contemplation also presupposes something else: namely, the fact that not only does the *act* of vision beyond death exist in a rudimentary, inchoate, premonitory form in this life, but also that the *object* of the beatific vision can be glimpsed, however imperfectly, by means of earthly contemplation. Because the world is a creation, *creatura,* God is present in it. The concept of a God wholly external to the world is not a Christian concept but the product of seventeenth and eighteenth century rationalism (the Enlightenment). God is not outside the world, and thus it is truly possible for him to reveal himself to a man whose gaze is turned upon the depths of things. This is a totally unromantic, purely diagnostic assertion. Only the vision of something we love makes us happy, and thus it is integral to the concept of contemplation that it represents a vision kindled by the act of turning towards something in love and affirmation. Given this fact, it is now possible for us to formulate a more complete definition of the essential meaning of contemplation. If we direct our power of affirmation, i.e., our love, toward the infinite and divine source of satiation which flows through all reality from its ultimate fount, and if this beloved source reveals itself to the gaze of the soul in a wholly unmediated and utterly serene vision—even if the vision persists for no more than a split second—then and only then does there occur what can, in an absolute sense, be called contemplation.

But perhaps it is more important to express this thought in positive terms and to say that when the aforementioned conditions are fulfilled, contemplation *always* occurs. For what seems to me particularly significant in the traditional theory of contemplation is the fact that this blissful awareness of the divine satiation of all desire can be kindled by any event, by the most trivial cause. Contemplation is by no means confined to the cloister and the monastic cell. The element crucial to contemplation can be attained by someone who does not even know the name for what is happening to him. Thus in all likelihood, contemplation occurs far more frequently than one would be led to believe by the prevailing image of modern man.

Not only do these inconspicuous forms of contemplation deserve more attention, more thought; they also deserve to be encouraged. We need to be expressly reassured of the fact that many of the experiences we have in the course of our day-to-day lives are in fact worthy of all the praise which has always been justly accorded to the contemplative life. We also need corroboration and confirmation of the fact that we are right to interpret and accept the beatitude of such experiences for what it truly is: the foretaste and beginning of perfect joy.

The time has come to speak of the contemplative mode of seeing the things of the Creation. I am referring to things which are perceptible to the senses, and to the kind of seeing we do with our eyes. It would be impossible to exaggerate the concreteness of this vision. If a person has been terribly thirsty for a long time and then finally drinks, feels the refreshment deep down inside and says, "What a glorious thing fresh, cold water is!"—then whether he knows it or not, he may have taken one step toward that beholding of the beloved wherein contemplation consists.

How splendid water is, or a rose, a tree, an apple! But as a rule we do not say such things, at least when we are in full possession of our faculties, without implying, to some degree, an affirmation which transcends the immediate object of our praise and the literal meaning of our words—an assent touching the foundation of the world. In the midst of our workaday cares we raise our heads and unexpectedly gaze into a face turned towards us, and in that instant we see: everything which is, is good, worthy of love, and loved by God.

At bottom all such certitudes invariably mean the same thing: The world is not out of joint after all; everything is moving toward its appointed end; despite everything there is peace, wholeness, and splendor in the depths of things; nothing and no one is lost; God (as Plato says) holds in his hands the beginning, the middle and the end of all things. But such proofs of the divine foundation and warranty of all Being —proofs which are not thought but *seen* and experienced directly—can be imparted to us when our gaze is directed at the most insignificant things, provided only that this gaze is kindled by love. This, in the most precise sense, is what is meant by contemplation, a contemplation which should dare to be what it is.

It is this kind of contemplation, born of the confrontation with the created word, which ceaselessly nourishes all true poetry and all genuine art, whose nature consists in praise, in a hymn of praise that transcends all lamentation. And no one who is incapable of such contemplation is capable of understanding poetry in the terms of poetry itself, in other words, in the only way which makes sense. The indispensable nature of art, its status as a basic necessity of human life, results above all from the fact that it prevents the contemplation of the

Creation from sinking into oblivion, and ensures that it remains a living force in our lives.

It seems appropriate at this point to speak of the journals of Gerard Manley Hopkins. They are filled with the testimony to earthly contemplation; in fact they speak of almost nothing else. This poet, who, despite the extreme refinement of his intellectual and spiritual sensibilities, is a compelling and even titanic figure, devoted a passionate attention to what he called the "inscapes" of the visible world. He did this not in order to achieve a pedantically realistic depiction of this world, but in order to become aware of, and to possess, the thousandfold riches of the works of God.

Thus he speaks of a flame "brighter and glossier than glass or silk or water", which "reeling up to the right in one long handkerchief and curling like a cartwhip", runs up a heap of dry honeysuckle; of the ridge of a hill "like a pale goldish skin without body"; of the cedar "laying level crow-feather strokes of boughs, with fine wave and dedication in them, against the light"; of the "sleeve of liquid barleyfield". One day in a field being used for military maneuvers he clearly perceived the "inscape of the horse" Sophocles had described in the lines of a chorus "running on the likeness of a horse to a breaker, a wave of the sea curling over". In the same manner, he speaks of the Rhône glacier, the flight of the heron, young elm leaves, a peacock's tail, and again and again of the shifting shapes of the clouds and of flowing water.

The precision of these notations reveals how unnecessary it is for the contemplative to "skip over" or to obliterate the reality of the visible by prematurely transforming it into some kind of "symbol". For his gaze is always directed straight at the heart of things. Of course, once one has achieved this depth of perception, an infinite network of relationships becomes visible which had hitherto remained concealed, and it is at this point that the essential act of contemplation comes to pass.

To be sure, no one has yet succeeded in adequately describing in words what it is that now appears before the eye of the soul. The glowing fire of the northern lights, which flare up independently of earthly chronology and appear "dated to the day of judgment", fill the entranced observer "with delighted fear". What vision was vouchsafed to him then? At another point Hopkins says, "I do not think I have ever seen anything more beautiful than the bluebell I have been looking at. I know the beauty of the Lord by it." What is the actual content of the message which became perceptible to him when he gazed at this blooming creation of God? He does not say a word about it. For this too belongs to the essence of all contemplation: the fact that it is incommunicable. It takes place in the innermost cell. No one can observe it. And it is impossible to "write the message down", for during the experience no faculty of the soul remains free and unengaged.

The glowing precision of Hopkins' depiction of sensory objects proves, as I have said, how profoundly the gaze of the earthly contemplative respects and seeks to preserve the visible element of the objects of the world. Perhaps the reverence for the concrete is actually stimulated by that contemplative impulse which seeks to penetrate the divine ground and meaning of all creatures and things. The aging Chesterton, reflecting on his past life, said that he had always felt an almost mystical conviction of the miracle in all that exists and of the rapture essentially inherent in all experience. This bold declaration implies several things: Every object shelters and conceals in its depth a sign of its divine origin. He who beholds it sees that this and all things else are good beyond all comprehension. He sees it and is happy.

This, in a nutshell, is the doctrine of earthly contemplation.

49

What Is a Feast?

Someone may remonstrate, "Does not everyone know what a festival is, anyhow?" The question is not altogether irrelevant. However, "If no one asks me, I know: if I wish to explain it to one that asks, I know not." This sentence from St. Augustine's *Confessions,* although written in relation to something else, is highly applicable to the concept of festivity. The problem is to put into words what everyone means and knows.

Nowadays, however, we are forcefully "asked" both what a festival is and, even more, what the psychological prerequisites are for celebrating one. "The trick is not to arrange a festival, but to find people who can *enjoy* it." The man who jotted down this aphorism nearly one hundred years ago was Friedrich Nietzsche; his genius, as this sentence once again illustrates, lay to no small degree in that seismographic sensitivity to what was to come. The implication is that festivity in general is in danger of extinction, for arrangements alone do not make a festival. . . .

But does not celebrating a festival mean simply the equivalent of having a good time? And does not everyone know what that is? Perhaps so—but again a few questions arise. What *is* a good time? Does anything of the sort exist? May it

In Tune with the World: A Theory of Festivity, pp. 10–24, translated by Richard and Clara Winston. © 1965 Harcourt, Brace & World. Reprinted with permission of Harcourt Brace Jovanovich, Inc. Originally published in German: *Zustimmung zur Welt,* 2nd edition. © 1964 by Kösel Verlag, Munich.

not be that the only kind of good time that is really possible is a time of good work?

These are questions we cannot answer unless we have a conception of man. For what is involved is the fulfillment of human life, and the form in which this fulfillment is to take place. Inevitably, therefore, we find ourselves concerned with such ideas as "the perfection of man", "eternal life", "bliss", "paradise". . . .

The traditional name for the utmost perfection to which man may attain, the fulfillment of his being, is *visio beatifica,* the "seeing that confers bliss". This is to say that the highest intensification of life, the absolutely perfect activity, the final stilling of all volition, and the partaking of the utmost fullness that life can offer takes place as a kind of seeing; more precisely, that all this is achieved in seeing awareness of the divine ground of the universe.

Incidentally, the tradition in which this view may be found extends much further back than the Christian centuries, perhaps back beyond historical time altogether. A few generations before Plato, the Greek Anaxagoras, in answer to the question of what he had been born for, replied: "For seeing." And in Plato's *Symposium* Diotima clearly expresses the traditional wisdom of the *visio beatifica*: "This is that life above all others which man should live, in the contemplation of divine beauty; this makes man immortal."

But eschatology alone is not the issue; the traditional wisdom does not speak only of the ultimate perfection of life in the "hereafter". It speaks also of man as an earthly being appearing in history, and asserts that man by nature craves the appeasement of his yearnings through seeing. In this present life also, the utmost happiness takes the form of contemplation. "Most of all we esteem the sense of sight", Aristotle says in the very beginning of his *Metaphysics*. And Pierre Teilhard de Chardin belongs to the same tradition when he suggests (in the remarkable chapter on vision which surprisingly opens his book, *The Phenomenon of Man*) that all life is comprehended within seeing, and that the whole evolution of the cosmos aims above all at "the elaboration of ever more perfect eyes". . . .

From this it follows that the concept of festivity is inconceivable without an element of contemplation. This does not mean exerting the argumentative intellect, but the "simple intuition" of reason; not the unrest of thought, but the mind's eye resting on whatever manifests itself. It means a relaxing of the strenuous fixation of the eye on the given frame of reference, without which no utilitarian act is accomplished. Instead, the field of vision widens, concern for success or failure of an act falls away, and the soul turns to its infinite object; it becomes aware of the illimitable horizon of reality as a whole. . . .

Bustle does not make a festival; on the contrary, it can spoil one. Of course this does not mean that a festival is simply contemplation and recollection of self; any such claim is clearly belied by experience. Nevertheless, we cling to the feeling that a special spice, essential to the right celebration of a festival, is a kind of expectant alertness. One must be able to look through and, as it were, beyond the immediate matter of the festival, including the festal gifts; one must engage in a listening, and therefore necessarily silent, meditation upon the fundament of existence. . . .

The antithesis between holiday and workday, or more precisely, the concept of the day of rest, tells us something further about the essence of festivity. The day of rest is not just a neutral interval inserted as a link in the chain of workaday life. It entails a loss of utilitarian profit. In voluntarily keeping the holiday, men renounce the yield of a day's labor. This renunciation has from time immemorial been regarded as an essential element of festivity. A definite span of usable time is made, as the ancient Romans understood it, "the exclusive property of the gods". As the animal for sacrifice was taken from the herd, so a piece of available time was expressly withdrawn from utility. The day of rest, then, meant not only that no work was done, but also that an offering was being made of the yield of labor. It is not merely that the time is not gainfully used; the offering is in the nature of a sacrifice, and therefore the diametric opposite of utility. . . .

This, then, unexpectedly brings us to a new aspect of a holiday. A festival is essentially a phenomenon of wealth; not, to be sure, the wealth of money, but of existential richness. Absence of calculation, in fact lavishness, is one of its elements. Of course there is a natural peril and a germ of degeneration inherent in this. The way is open to senseless and excessive waste of the yield of work, to an extravagance that violates all rationality. The product of a whole year's labor can be thrown away on a single day. As is well known, men are quite capable of such behavior. But this potential perversion cannot be included within the definition of festivity, as has recently been done. We may properly say that every festival conceals within itself "at least a germ of excess"; but it is highly misleading if festival itself is defined as *le paroxysme de la société,* as a submergence in "creative" chaos. True enough, the fact remains that the paramountcy of a calculating, economizing mentality prevents both festive excess and festivity itself. In the workaday world all magnificence and pomp is calculated, and therefore unfestive. The myriad lights of a commercialized Christmas inevitably seem basically meager, without any real radiance. We remember G. K. Chesterton's keen comment on the dazzling advertisements of Times Square at night: what a glorious sight for those who luckily do not know how to read.

Such an act of renunciation and sacrificial offering, however, cannot be imagined as being performed at random. The talk of "valuable working time" is, after all, not just talk; something utterly real is involved. Why should anyone decide to sacrifice this precious article without sufficient reason? If we probe a little more insistently for a reason, we find a curious analogy to the other, the contemplative aspect of the day of rest, of which we have already spoken. The achievement of contemplation, since it is the seeing, the intuition of the beloved object, presupposes a specific nonintellectual, direct, and existential relation to reality, an existential concord of man with the world and with himself. Precisely in the same way, the act of freely giving oneself cannot take place unless it likewise grows from the root of a comprehensive affirmation—for which no other term can be found than "love". In spite of the thickets of banality, sentimentality and unrealistic spiritualization that threaten to smother the true meaning of this word, it remains indispensable. There is no other word that so precisely denotes what is at issue.

We do not renounce things, then, except for love. . . . Joy is an expression of love. One who loves nothing and nobody cannot possibly rejoice, no matter how desperately he craves joy. Joy is the response of a lover receiving what he loves. . . .

The inner structure of real festivity has been stated in the clearest and tersest possible fashion by Chrysostom: *ubi caritas gaudet, ibi est festivitas;* "where love rejoices, there is festivity".

Now, what sort of reason underlies festal joy and therefore festivity itself? . . . It is an almost equally hopeless simplification to imagine that mere ideas can be the occasion for real festivals. Something more is needed, something of another order. The celebrant himself must have shared in a distinctly real experience. When Easter is declared a festival of "immortality", it is scarcely surprising that no response is forthcoming —not to speak of such fantastic proposals as those of Auguste Comte, whose reformed calendar established festivals of Humanity, Paternity and even Domesticity. Not even the idea of freedom can inspire people with a spirit of festivity, though the celebration of liberation might—assuming that the event, though possibly belonging to the distant past, still has compelling contemporary force. Memorial days are not in themselves festival days. Strictly speaking, the past cannot be celebrated festively unless the celebrant community still draws glory and exaltation from that past, not merely as reflected history, but by virtue of a historical reality still operative in the present. If the Incarnation of God is no longer understood as an event that directly concerns the present lives of men, it becomes impossible, even absurd, to celebrate Christmas festively.

Josef Andreas Jungmann has recently suggested that festivals as an institution have already become derivative, whereas the "prototypal form" of festival still takes place where a specific event such as birth, marriage, or homecoming is being directly celebrated. If the implication is that the specific event is the real reason of all celebrations, and also the highest rationale which a modern theory of festivals can provide, the thesis is not altogether convincing. We can and must pursue the inquiry further, to ask, for example: On what grounds does a specific event become the occasion for festival and celebration? Can we festively celebrate the birth of a child if we hold with Jean-Paul Sartre's dictum: "It is absurd that we are born"? Anyone who is seriously convinced that "our whole existence is something that would be better not being", and that consequently life is not worth living, can no more celebrate the birth of his child than any other birthday, his own or anyone else's, a fiftieth or sixtieth or any other. No single specific event can become the occasion for festive celebrations unless—unless what?

Here is where we must be able to name the reason underlying all others, the "reason why" events such as birth, marriage, homecoming are felt as the receiving of something beloved, without which there can be neither joy nor festivity. Again we find Nietzsche expressing the crucial insight—one painfully brought home, it would seem, as the result of terrible inner trials, for he was as familiar with the despair of being unable to take "enough joy in anything" as with "the vast unbounded Yea- and Amen-saying". The formulation is to be found in his posthumous notes, and reads: "To have joy in anything, one must approve everything."

Underlying all festive joy kindled by a specific circumstance there has to be an absolutely universal affirmation extending to the world as a whole, to the reality of things and the existence of man himself. . . . For man cannot have the experience of receiving what is loved, unless the world and existence as a whole represent something good and therefore beloved to him. . . .

Need we bother to say how little such affirmation has to do with shallow optimism, let alone with smug approval of that which is? Such affirmation is not won by deliberately shutting one's eyes to the horrors in this world. Rather, it proves its seriousness by its confrontation with historical evil. The quality of this assent is such that we must attribute it even to martyrs, at the very moment, perhaps, that they perish under brutal assault. A theologian commenting on the Apocalypse has said that what distinguishes the Christian martyr is that he never utters a word against God's Creation. In spite of everything he finds the things that are "very good"; therefore in spite of everything he remains capable of joy and even, as far as it concerns him, of festivity. Whereas, on the other hand, whoever refuses assent to reality as a whole, no matter how well off he may be, is by that fact incapacitated for either joy or festivity. Festivity is impossible to the nay-sayer. The more money he has, and above all the more leisure, the more desperate is this impossibility to him. . . .

Festivity lives on affirmation. Even celebrations for the dead, All Souls and Good Friday, can never be truly celebrated except on the basis of faith that all is well with the world and life as a whole. If there is no consolation, the idea of a funeral as a solemn act is self-contradictory. But consolation is a form of rejoicing, although the most silent of all—just as catharsis, the purification of the soul in the witnessing of tragedy, is at bottom a *joyful* experience. (The real locus of the tragic is not in those works of literature we term tragedies, but in man's historical reality.) Consolation exists only on the premise that grief, sorrow, death, are accepted, and therefore affirmed, as meaningful in spite of everything.

This is the point at which to correct the misconception which sometimes prevails, that the festive is also the cheerful.

. . . It is true that a festival becomes true festivity only when man affirms the goodness of his existence by offering the response of joy. Can it be that this goodness is never revealed to us so brightly and powerfully as by the sudden shock of loss and death? This is the implication of Hölderlin's famous distich (on Sophocles' *Antigone*):

> *Viele versuchten umsonst, das Freudigste freudig zu sagen,*
> *Hier spricht endlich es mir, hier in der Trauer sich aus.*

> Many endeavored in vain joyfully to speak profoundest joy;
> Here at last, in the tragic, I see it expressed.

Is it therefore so surprising that both the affirmation of life and its rejection should be hard to recognize, not only to the eye of the outsider but possibly to one's own inner eye? . . .

Strictly speaking, however, it is insufficient to call affirmation of the world a mere prerequisite and premise for festivity. In fact it is far more; it is the substance of festivity. Festivity, in its essential core, is nothing but the living out of this affirmation.

To celebrate a festival means: to live out, for some special occasion and in an uncommon manner, the universal assent to the world as a whole . . . .

First of all, we must now state explicitly a conclusion toward which all our foregoing ideas have inexorably led. To be sure, as I have found time and again, this statement is usually greeted with alarm and distrust, as though to voice it is somehow equivalent to launching an unfair surprise attack. Nevertheless, I see no legitimate way of avoiding it; it is absolutely compelling, both logically and existentially.

The conclusion is divisible into several parts. *First:* there can be no more radical assent to the world than the praise of God, the lauding of the Creator of this same world. One cannot conceive a more intense, more unconditional affirmation of being. If the heart of festivity consists in men's physically ex-

pressing their agreement with everything that is, then—
secondly—the ritual festival is the most festive form that festivity can possibly take. The other side of this coin is that—
thirdly—there can be no deadlier, more ruthless destruction of
festivity than refusal of ritual praise. Any such Nay tramples
out the spark from which the flickering flame of festivity
might have been kindled anew.

Truths—Known and Believed

50

Knowing and Believing

Truth is the self-manifestation and state of evidence of real things. Consequently, truth is something secondary, following from something else. Truth does not exist for itself alone. Primary and precedent to it are existing things, the real. Knowledge of truth, therefore, aims ultimately not at "truth" but, strictly speaking, at gaining sight of reality. Furthermore, when we distinguish "truth of faith" from "truth of reason", we are saying that on the one hand there exist things which we can see only by faith and divine revelation, and on the other hand things which can be apprehended by natural cognition. Even when we speak of "faith" and "knowledge", despite the literal meaning of these words we are not speaking of two different acts or approaches of the human mind, but of two realms of reality which we touch upon when we believe or know.

"Conjunction of faith and knowledge" — at bottom that comes down to mentally uniting these two *realms of reality:* on the one hand the totality of created things which lie within the purview of natural cognition (which does not mean that we ever fully understand them); and on the other hand the reality exposed to us in God's revelations, that is to say, in faith. For this latter reality, we have the code words "Trinity" and "Incarnation". To interpret the conjunction in this way,

Scholasticism: Personalities and Problems of Medieval Philosophy, pp. 118–19, translated by Richard and Clara Winston. © 1960 Pantheon Books, Inc., New York. Used with permission.

however, is also to make a demand that is not directed at the rational intellect alone: to this extent the expression "mentally uniting" is not quite accurate. For what we are called upon to do is not entirely mental; it lies closer to the core of personality than that, and challenges spiritual existence.

This, then, is more or less the interpretation that Thomas Aquinas gave to Boethius' celebrated dictum. It was the most radical formulation which could be given to the idea. With that consistency absolutely distinctive in him, Thomas sees natural reality as divine creation which in the event of the Incarnation has been reunited, in an incomprehensibly new way, with its Origin.

And in seeing and saying this, he makes two things plain: first, that man's turning toward all aspects of the world is an attitude not only justified but required by theology—very much so; and second, that theology itself can develop only within the framework of total reality, and that not one single element of that total reality can be excluded from consideration. As we summed it up once before: "theologically based worldliness, and a theology open to the world".

51

"Theology" without Faith

The "difficulty in having faith", of course, did not arise just "today"; it has always been around—what else should we expect? After all, our human mind by its very nature demands to experience things and be convinced through compelling ar-

Originally published in *Über die Schwierigkeit, heute zu glauben* (Munich: Kösel-Verlag, 1974). Translated by Lothar Krauth.

guments. Faith, however, asks to accept something as true and real, not based on firsthand knowledge of a situation but on the testimony of someone else. The one who believes expects this "someone else" not to be simply another believer but someone who has seen and knows. Regarding religious and revealed faith there arises an even more acute difficulty. For the witness and authority, on whose word the believer relies, is none other than God himself whom we do not meet directly. Nevertheless, because such faith, of course, does not and must not simply happen somewhere in thin air, it becomes understandable why disagreements and disputes in this area appear to be unavoidable.

And yet the "difficulty in having faith" manifests itself nowadays with distinctive characteristics and new reasons. This is the moment to mention the "devastation of theology". True, this expression was coined a century and a half ago by Hegel in the last decade of his life. But its relevance applies disturbingly to our present time as well. This expression aims at the enlightened and agnostic Bible scholar and at a "theology" without faith. Georges Bernanos, in the title of an almost prophetic novel, has called such a theology by its true name and stated its real identity as "deception". It is precisely this deception that "today" threatens effectively to block the opportunity for the "common man" to find it possible to believe. I am unable, of course, to share Hegel's opinion that the "devastation" wrought by a pseudotheology could be remedied through the power of philosophical reason. Nevertheless I am convinced that here a task awaits the philosopher that nobody else would be able to fulfill.

The great teachers of Christianity have in ever-new formulations expressed the thought that grace does not destroy nature but rather builds on it and brings it to perfection. This thought, springing from a specifically theological world view and therefore ignored by those fashionable pseudotheologies, implies for example that any acceptance in faith of God's revelation presupposes certain truths already established in our mind, truths that can be attained by mere natural reason.

These truths have to be "established", meaning: that we not simply know them but willingly embrace them and thus incorporate them into our personal mental make-up.

Pseudotheology highhandedly determines its own domain and proclaims to be its own master. True theology is well aware of its obligation to respect the antecedent norm of divine revelation while at the same time recognizing its need for the partnership of an unbiased approach to the reality of nature. Furthermore, you can penetrate its inner sanctum only through an antechamber. Whoever does not appreciate the significance of signs and symbols will never understand the essence of a sacrament, and only those who realize what constitutes a sacred action will find the way open to a deeper understanding of the Christian cultus and mystery.

The borderline, of course, between antechamber and inner sanctum must not be blurred. It is important to preserve the distinction between philosophy and theology. And yet their strict separation from each other seems to me not only virtually impossible but above all illicit; for in that process each would be left sterile.

52

Philosophy out of a Christian Existence

I am convinced that, without exception, every philosophical interpretation of the world and human existence relies, at least subconsciously, on certain general assumptions which are not so much "knowledge" as rather "belief". The following re-

---

Originally published in *Verteidigungsrede für die Philosophie* (Munich: Kösel-Verlag, 1966). Translated by Lothar Krauth.

flections will nonetheless consider only those situations in which the philosopher is also explicitly a believer who openly accepts the truth of a sacred tradition and consciously tries to be aware of it in his reasoning. Such a believer, in a Western cultural context, will more than likely be a Christian. True, Christian doctrine is primarily concerned with offering salvation, not with interpreting reality or human existence. But it implies as well certain fundamental teachings on specifically philosophical matters—the world and existence as such.

Our thesis, then, to be considered here, states in particular: To claim existential honesty as a Christian philosopher, you cannot disregard the truths of divine revelation that you have accepted in faith.

We are not considering philosophy "as such" here; rather the existential approach to philosophy and the person of the philosopher. The question here, therefore, is not whether a systematic discourse on philosophical problems should also admit theological statements or not. It may well be that even this question should not be answered with a simple "no". But this is not the topic of our discussion here. The topic is the following contention: suppose a philosopher has personally accepted as true certain preter-rational statements on reality and existence; that is, he does not entertain any doubt about their truth, though not uncritically or naïvely. Suppose further that he explicitly disregards this conviction of his in his philosophical discourse. He would then immediately cease to be an honest philosopher, because from that moment on he would no longer consider his subject matter, the world and existence as such, "under every conceivable aspect".

In the philosophical literature of our time two important voices are raised, each for its own reason, against this assertion; both, however, are highly representative: the voices of Martin Heidegger and Karl Jaspers.

Heidegger states that anyone who accepts the biblical creation account as truth will always remain "a stranger to the primordial force" of philosophical questioning because he already claims to possess the answer to the question—indeed, the answer to the one question that constitutes philosophy as such: Why is there anything at all and not, rather, nothing? "The very content of our question is folly to the faith. Philosophy consists in this folly. A 'Christian philosophy' is a wooden iron and a misconception."

Jaspers asserts as well that religious faith and philosophy are incompatible, though—as mentioned—for a different reason: no "honest person can escape the choice between religion and philosophy; it's either renouncing independence, or renouncing revelation". Faith here is conceived, entirely correctly, as total trust in someone whose authority I acknowledge. Precisely this attitude, however, would not be permissible for the philosopher. "Authority is the specific enemy of philosophy"; any reason adduced to justify submission to an authority "renounces freedom". All this, I should quickly add, shows only a partial aspect of Jaspers' much more differentiated total conception of the relationship between philosophy and religion. ("Philosophy, in fact, springs from the soil of a religious substance whose explicit manifestation it simultaneously opposes.") Yet the dimension pertinent to our context here is clearly and definitely part of his thinking.

Put in a nutshell, all this reads: A believer cannot also be a philosopher, and vice versa: a philosopher cannot be a believer. On closer examination of the way philosophy is implicitly conceived and defined in these propositions, we discover a somewhat strange fact: both theses emphasize a certain aspect that was hardly relevant, if present at all, in the accepted idea of philosophy from Plato to Kant.

First, however, we return to Heidegger's position, which after all raises some further intriguing questions. Does he not fail to grasp the very essence of faith? Faith, indeed, implies precisely the absence of assured knowledge and possession, in spite of all "revelation". This is why the theologian speaks of the "truths of faith" that "nevertheless remain hidden". And regarding "the single" philosophical question of "Why is there anything at all?"—this question, through revelation and faith rather accentuated than silenced, assumes its utmost weight and urgency in view of the totally "uncaused" divine Being. But here we cannot pursue this further. Our interest, rather, centers on the radical challenge of Heidegger's insistence on philosophy as "absolute questioning". "To endure—questioning, defenseless—amidst the uncertainty of *being* as such", he even claims, would be "the highest form of knowledge".

At this point one might perhaps look up in surprise and reply with the question: Am I myself not saying exactly the same thing? Have I not already explicitly discussed philosophy's intrinsic structure of hope as well as the questioning reflection on reality as such, a questioning that can never be stilled by any final or exhaustive answer? Yes, I have. Any similarity, nonetheless, exists only in appearance. The difference, to put it bluntly and somewhat aggressively, lies in this: for me, "questioning" means to be aware of the elusiveness of any final answer yet nevertheless to pursue such an answer and remain open to it. For Heidegger, in contrast, "questioning" seems to mean the absolute exclusion and rejection of any possible answer (which answer, in fact, would infringe on the purity of questioning itself).

Karl Jaspers' position, too, presents problems in several respects. I ask myself, for instance, what "renouncing revelation" might possibly mean—after all, does "revelation" not mean that God has spoken to man? But we cannot pursue this question, either. We are concerned here with Jaspers' specific conception of philosophy. It seems to be distinguished by its emphasis on the philosopher's independence. The philosopher, of course, is definitely searching for answers, yet not so absolutely as to be willing to accept them from someone else. This emphasis, I believe, is not entirely absent in the traditional conception of philosophy, but it is nearly irrelevant there.

Both positions, Jaspers' as well as Heidegger's, have in common a downright jealous vigilance regarding the purity and integrity of the formal approach to philosophy. The "purity" of the philosophical method seems to be almost more important than the answer to the philosophical question itself. In precisely this lies its difference from the thinking in the mainstream of Western philosophy. We may almost assert that Plato and Aristotle, in this sense, entirely lacked interest in "philosophy", at least as regards a clearly and formally defined academic discipline, and were not at all concerned with borderlines as such. Instead, their relentlessly probing minds were totally engaged in an attempt to bring into view and define the ultimate nature of human virtue, of *eros*, of reality in general. Their inquiry was directed by no other concern than the search for answers to these questions — be those answers ever so vulnerable and fragmentary, and above all: no matter what quarter they came from! Socrates, in Plato's writings, was never embarrassed to admit that the ultimate, the ontologically decisive truths were known to him not by his own accomplishments but *ex akoés*, "because he heard them". And the proximity of the rational argument to the mythic tradition, a distinctive feature of nearly all of Plato's *Dialogues*, means exactly the same. In Aristotle's much more "scientific" philosophy such a willingness to listen to preter-rational answers is less evident. Yet it has convincingly been shown that "his metaphysics, too, imply the principle of *credo ut intelligam* [I believe in order to understand]". Even Immanuel Kant still stands in this very same tradition, though similarly not in blatant and explicit terms. Thus it comes as quite a surprise to hear him, eight years after *The Critique of Pure Reason*, when he calls the New Testament "an everlasting guide to true wisdom" from which our mind "receiveth new light in contemplating those things which our mind faileth to grasp yet always needeth for its instruction".

How, then, would the correlation between knowledge and faith be a concrete part of the philosophical discourse, and how could it be formally and theoretically defined? This is a further and extremely complicated question; still, we shall consider it at least briefly.

We stated so far that the philosopher who is existentially also a believer would have to "respect" the truths of divine revelation, would have to "include" and "consider" them. At the very least he must not "ignore" them nor "isolate" them from his reasoning. These expressions may indeed be helpful approximations. Yet possibly they tend to obscure the infinite difficulty inherent in any attempt to legitimize the connection between the two realms of inquiry. The distinction between knowledge and faith remains essentially unbridged; these are clearly two different things that we try to connect in such a way that each preserves its own form and dignity. There can be no question, therefore, of any homogeneous intermingling of the two. On the other hand, though, the notion of a methodically exact delineation of their respective turf, and thus the notion of "border violation", remains quite atypical for the philosopher as well as the theologian, should it appear at all. Neither the one nor the other is entitled to claim every other scientist's obvious prerogative and say, "This is of interest to me, that is not." For both must invariably deal with the "universal, with totality, with things divine and human". Right from the start, then, we must brace ourselves for almost insurmountable difficulties in any attempt to describe adequately the specifics of the connection in question here.

In this we should not despise symbolic images. A truly striking analogy has the advantage of presenting to the inner eye a simple image without destroying the *arcanum* [mystery] that indeed permeates all reality.

To explain the correlation of knowledge and faith, the image of a polyphonic counterpoint immediately makes sense. In such a composition, independent melodies correlate with each other, accentuate, challenge, perhaps even disturb each other in such a way as to create a fresh, rich and captivating harmony that can no longer be explained by merely adding together its individual components.

It may well be more than merely an "image" to call the believer "a listener". Is there any way to express it more accurately? A believer neither "knows" nor "sees" with his own eyes; he accepts the testimony of someone else. Much of this testimony, indeed, regards the same universe that his own eyes behold, and that he, as scientist and philosopher, investigates using his own faculties. Such testimony may even guide his attention or sharpen his perception so that he suddenly sees with his own eyes what otherwise would have remained hidden, had he not heeded and pondered the message reaching him from elsewhere. The clarifying power of such an image is evident. It makes quite clear, for example, that Karl Jaspers' inescapable alternative of faith or philosophy is entirely nonexistent. Why should I be compelled to choose in favor of "hearing" and against the use of my own eyes, and vice versa? What could prevent me from accepting both: seeing and hearing, philosophy and faith? And then, who could ever determine the pattern and structure according to which knowing and believing also mix and intermingle in the common everyday activity of the human mind?

In fact, nowhere is it written that explicit rules for the correlation of knowledge and faith may be possible at all. What is more, we face here more than just a theoretical difficulty. Such a correlation needs to be lived, and this within the infinitely variable context of a concrete existence. Conflicts here are not only possible but downright inevitable, as the natural concomitants of mental progress. We may even go so far as to recognize the mark of a truly philosophical attitude whenever such conflicts are serenely faced and patiently endured, without the ready inclination toward hasty harmonization or premature capitulation. The statement comes to mind that says that a philosophy embracing truly all attainable information is superior, not because it would be able to offer smoother answers but because it will bring out more clearly the dimension of mystery that pervades all reality.

In the end it may not be overly important to search for a theoretical formula that would assign with utmost accuracy its specific function to faith, knowledge and philosophy alike. It is more decisive to live out that unrestrained, all-embracing openness that is not so much an attitude or virtue of the human mind but rather its very essence, its nature itself.

53

The Possible Future of Philosophy

Nowadays when we use the word "future" — and indeed we tend to use it rather too often — it may have a variety of implications, or at least of nuances and overtones. Its meaning depends on the context. For example, anyone who compares the two phrases "the future of space travel" and "man and his future", will be instantly sensible of the fact that in these two cases, the word "future" has a very different ring to it. The first phrase conveys an element of triumphant confidence, whereas the second is characterized rather by a tone of doubt and anxiety. This same note of anxiety is always struck when people discuss the future of philosophy, and perhaps for much the same reasons. After all, the future of philosophy is presumably dependent on the future of man. I fear that when many people hear someone speak of the "future of philosophy", the image that comes to their minds is that of a terminally ill patient to whom his friends persist in talking about "tomorrow" or even "next spring".

T. S. Eliot actually speaks of the "sickness of philosophy, an obscure recognition of which moves those who complain

Problems of Modern Faith, pp. 265–76, translated by Jan van Heurck. © 1985 Franciscan Herald Press, Chicago. Reprinted with permission.

of its decline". This sickness, Eliot continues, "has been present too long to be attributable to any particular contemporary school of thought". He himself sees "the root cause" of the evil in the divorce of philosophy from theology. If Eliot is right — and I am convinced that at least certain elements of the contemporary crisis in philosophy in fact represent nothing more than the logical consequence of this "divorce" — then the future of philosophy depends on whether or not its isolation from theology is something which can legitimately be overcome. However, one cannot answer or even discuss this question unless one first possesses a reasonably clear idea of what sort of "marriage" between philosophy and theology is feasible or desirable. For, as there is really no need to point out, certain forms of alliance between philosophy and theology are, in an irrevocable sense, "past history". For example, it is highly improbable that the philosophical discipline of logic will ever again be inspired, as it was in Abelard's day, by the theological problem of a God who is at the same time One and Triune. Moreover, any discussion of a possible "remarriage" between philosophy and theology will necessarily involve the question of what kind of theology we have in mind. And what do we mean by "theology" in general? It may well be true that only theology itself can provide us with a valid definition of theology. Nevertheless, in my opinion the philosopher cannot afford to ignore or neglect the question of the nature of theology, insofar as it represents a potential activity of the intellect. I would like to comment briefly on this issue before proceeding further.

The philosopher, or as I would prefer to call him, the "philosophizer" or the person who engages in the philosophical act, is not so much someone who has succeeded in working out a finished, seamless view of the world as he is someone who occupies himself with keeping alive a certain question: the question of the ultimate meaning of reality as a whole. No doubt he is capable of discovering a series of provisional answers to this question, but never "the" answer. His effort to grasp what Alfred North Whitehead calls the "complete fact" necessarily constitutes a task which can never be completed. What happens when a human being dies—not merely in physiological terms or in terms of his personal history, but viewed from every possible aspect? What really takes place in an act of cognition? What does it mean to speak of something as "real"? No one will ever be able to supply an adequate answer to any of these questions. And yet the specific task of philosophy is precisely to ensure that human beings remain alert and responsive to this unfathomable thing, the "complete fact", to arouse their distrust of any claim by any person that he has found the "key to the universe", to resist every premature attempt to reduce the world to a harmonious system by suppressing, or failing to take into account, so much as one single element of reality as a whole.

But the philosopher is not alone. There is someone standing at his side, someone who has always been there, someone who, like the philosopher, speaks about the totality of the world and existence. However, this man—or so it appears—speaks of this totality not so much by posing disquieting questions as by giving voice to an unhesitatingly affirmative *answer*. This second man is the theologian. What he has to say goes something like this: The world and man are created beings. In other words, all existing things, including man himself, derive their internal structure from a design which issued from the creative realization of an absolute intellect. Moreover, man is not only a created being, *creatura,* but he is actually the image of the Creator—and so on. One thing is immediately apparent: Assertions of this kind deal with precisely the same theme with which philosophy, by definition, deals: namely, the ultimate meaning of the world and existence as a whole.

For the philosopher it is a significant moment when he first becomes aware of the presence of this other man at his side, who apparently has been there all along. From this moment on, the person who engaged in the philosophical act is compelled to define his own trade with greater precision and to draw a clear distinction between it and the trade of the theologian. The process of defining the respective territories of the philosopher and the theologian has been going on from time out of mind. For it is the necessity of reflecting on his relationship to the theologian which alone enables the philosopher to gain a clearer understanding of the nature of his own task. But of course there is much more to this "moment of confrontation" than I have indicated so far.

For example, it is not entirely correct to describe the theologian as "someone else", as the "second man". At least he does not always necessarily fit this description. And in the beginning, the theologian is in fact *not* "someone else" at all. At the beginning of human history, as well as at the beginning of each individual human life, philosophy and theology are not divorced, but are one. Every person who asks the meaning of the world and existence as a whole begins as a believer. Of course the process of differentiation, of distinguishing between himself and what is "other", begins the first time he engages in a critical act of philosophical reflection—even if this is only the act of distinguishing between two different acts of the same person. This process of differentiation is both inevitable and highly significant, for it reveals that there are in fact two different ways of thinking and talking about the same world, the world which is lying right before our eyes. Moreover, these two ways of thinking and talking also employ two different methods to establish their credentials and justify their contentions. As the philosopher reflects on the particular question which concerns him, he keeps his gaze fixed on the empirical world; like the scientist, he uses his own eyes. And whatever his philosophical conclusions may be, he must prove their validity by checking them out against experience. On the other hand, by virtue of its intrinsic logical structure, the theologian's job is far more complex and problematical, as well as far more derivative, i.e., "secondhand". It presupposes far more than the mere existence of an empirical reality "out there" before his eyes. When, for example, the theologian speaks of man as made in the image of God, or of the world as a created thing, *creatura,* he is not basing his assertion on something which he himself sees and knows. Instead he is relying on a divine communication which can in no way be inferred or deduced from the empirical reality of the world and of man. In short, there can be no theology if there is no such thing as revelation, in the strict sense of the term. Theology is nothing other than the attempt to interpret the documents of divine revelation preserved by sacred tradition. This "interpretation" does not primarily involve textual criticism, but rather the effort to determine, with the greatest possible precision, the probable *sensus divinus,* or divine meaning, of a text which of course has been conditioned by a wide variety of historical factors. Thus, by this definition, theology is a *human* endeavor through and through. Of course we can conceive of one highly significant exception to this rule, an exception which in fact is more than merely "conceivable", so that perhaps it is not strictly correct to speak of it as an "exception". I am referring to the possibility that the Author of the revelation may himself inspire its interpretation. That he in fact does so is the presupposition of "theology" in the sense of *doctrina sacra.* However, we are not discussing this kind of theology at the moment. Instead we are considering theology as an exclusively human enterprise.

But our strictly "human" theologian is incapable of exercising his proper, distinctive trade unless he is prepared to cooperate with science and philosophy. It is, quite simply, impermissible that he restrict himself, in analyzing the documents of revelation, to scriptural exegesis in the narrowest sense. For example, how could a contemporary theologian hope to interpret the biblical account of the Creation if he ignores his obligation to reflect, with the greatest seriousness, on the conclusions of paleontologists and the results of modern research into evolution? The reason for this obligation is *not* that a modern theologian ought to be "up to date" in scientific as well as theological matters. No, the reason is that unless he meets this obligation, he will, quite simply, be incapable of carrying out his specific task *as a theologian*. This task consists in making plausible to his contemporaries the idea that it still has meaning—and then specifying *what* meaning it has—to say: "God formed man of the dust of the ground, and breathed into his nostrils the breath of life" (Gen 2:7).

"Interpretation" always involves a form of translation, a transposition of meaning from one language into another. Thus it is integral to the formal structure of a theological proposition that it "materializes", so to speak, in two distinct languages. One language is the specific mentality of that generation of human beings to whom the theologian must make comprehensible the words of revelation and sacred tradition —to whom he must reveal that these words constitute information about the world and existence which still has meaning, and discloses reality, in the here and now.

By the way, there are many indications that this view of the nature of theology is specifically "Western" or "Occidental", for apparently no such notion exists either in Hinduism or Islam. In any case, whenever a theologian undertakes this bold adventure—the adventure of engaging in a contrapuntal cooperation with scientists in their ever-expanding investigations of reality, and with philosophers in their ever-changing attempts to interpret existence—theology becomes subject to demands which it is well-nigh impossible to meet. Certainly it is beyond the powers of any single individual to meet them, no matter how great his genius. For example, once he has accepted the obligations of such a cooperative or collaborative effort, it becomes impossible for the theologian to limit the area of his concern to what appears "relevant to theological issues". Thomas Aquinas would point out that no one is competent to judge beforehand what knowledge will prove important (i.e., "relevant") or unimportant to the theologian. However, the theologian faces far graver difficulties than this, for the "cooperation" in which he has chosen to engage in no way resembles a more or less academic "dialogue" between theology on the one hand and science and philosophy on the other. As a rule it is far more likely to take the form of a fierce and relentless armed confrontation in which the opponents no longer appear to have any common ground. And yet, once again, if he is to carry out his own highly specialized task, the theologian is *not* authorized to withdraw from the debate. An examination of the history of theology reveals that the more profound disclosure of the meaning of the Word of God very rarely resulted from the peaceful, autonomous development of a theology left to its own devices. Far more often progress resulted from rigorous confrontation. Nevertheless, it would be incorrect to claim that advances in theology are achieved solely as the result of pressures exerted from outside. Instead we owe these advances to the fact that theologians themselves regarded it as their duty to engage in painful and perplexing confrontations. We cannot describe the flux of theological thought in terms of botanical categories ("growth", "development", "blossoming"). In reality the elaboration of theological truth is a distinctively *human* process involving freedom, choice, guilt, the susceptibility to error and the potential for corruption, as well as all those painful challenges which normally accompany and, so to speak, induce, ethical maturation.

In order to ply his trade, the theologian must be prepared to face conflicts of this kind. Theology must inevitably remain sterile unless theologians are willing to endure the pain of opposition and discordant views. John Henry Newman described in no uncertain terms some of the typical "perversions" of theology: the love of system and theorizing, fancifulness, dogmatism, bigotry and, as a result of these, sectarianism, sophistry and the denunciation of others." The "office" which science and philosophy are called on to render to theology is, above all, to prevent theology from taking refuge in the illusion that it is self-sufficient. Even the notorious description of philosophy as the *ancilla theologiae*, the handmaid of theology, which has been misinterpreted a thousand times by theologians and philosophers alike, ultimately implies nothing more than the necessity of collaboration between the two disciplines. Theology *needs* contact with philosophy and science—and naturally with an *independent* philosophy and an *autonomous* science.

But now the time has come to look at the other side of the coin, i.e., the role of philosophy. For it is not only theology which profits from the collaboration of which we have been speaking. The person who engages in the philosophical act acquires something from the contact with theology which he could acquire nowhere else and in no other way. But the reward he acquires has two aspects, just as it does for the theologian: that of enrichment and that of disquiet.

For example, the philosopher who also has faith—who regards the world as a creation which issued from the divine Logos and which, although it is fundamentally luminous, lucid, clear and bright, *at the same time* reflects a design which by its very nature is inaccessible to human understanding—only a philosopher like this is in a position to divine how the knowability of the world and its incomprehensibility (both of which attributes are more or less demonstrable by empirical methods) could derive from the same root. This insight, which is clearly philosophical in nature in that it derives from the encounter with empirical reality, can nevertheless be imparted only to a person who is prepared to learn from theology something which he could never come to know on his own. Of course, the greatest enrichment which the philosopher can derive from the collaboration with theology lies in the fact that it can prevent him from falling prey to those dangers inherent in philosophy itself, the chief among which is the natural desire to create a clear, transparent and unified image of the world. For example, the idea of the Incarnation of God, in which the ultimate work of the creation was linked with the origin of that creation to form a circle, might appeal to a "Gnostic" philosopher who saw in it the unlooked-for confirmation of a world view based on a single all-embracing principle. But the facts that, within the framework, mankind hated and killed the God-made-man "without a cause" (Jn 15:25) and that yet this same death effected the salvation of man, who had committed the murder: these theological truths explode any tidy formula which anyone might conceive about the world. Another example: A philosophy of history which takes into account the possibility of a catastrophic end to history within time and yet, on the grounds of the same apocalyptic theology, is opposed to the conclusion, born of despair, that existence is therefore absurd, must inevitably prove far more arduous, more complex, and, so to speak, "less satisfying" than any philosophy of progress (whether based on idealist, Marxist, or evolutionary conceptions) or any metaphysics of decline and fall [both of which are unilateral in character]. Thus the person who engages in the philosophical act appears to derive a certain *handicap* from his collaboration with theology, but simultaneously he derives an enrichment which can be summed up in the term: higher truth. For the essential thing in philosophy is neither the avoidance of knotty problems nor the bewitchment of the intellect with plausible or conclusive proofs. Instead the essential thing is that not one single element of reality be suppressed or concealed—not one element of that unfathomable reality the vision of which is synonymous with the concept of "truth".

In the interests of fairness we must, in conclusion, say something about the typical perversions of a philosophy which rejects any partnership with theology, [just as we described the perversions of a theology which refuses contact with philosophy]. Naturally, I am not referring here to any philosopher who has never had the slightest inkling of the possibility of collaboration between his discipline and theology. Instead I am speaking only of philosophers who deliberately reject and refuse to engage in such collaboration. One could easily name a whole series of philosophical perversions which result from this attitude. Pride of place is held by a purely formalistic intellectual "game playing" which may well be of a very high quality and which, like all other forms of "entertainment", presupposes the existence of a widespread intellectual boredom and relies principally on the creation of surprise effects. This kind of philosophy exemplifies what Hegel called "the vanity of opinions". A more pernicious result of the rejection by philosophy of any tie with an authentic theology is the fact that the exponents of such a philosophy almost inevitably end up regarding it as a "doctrine of salvation" and manifest all the symptoms which are usually attendant upon such a view: mystagogical terminology and ritual, the formation of bodies of disciples, intolerance toward other views and so on. A philosophy which has discarded the substance of the great (Western) intellectual tradition suffers from a secret flaw. The most ruthless and pitiless indictment of this flaw was spoken by Karl Jaspers when he said that the hallmark of such a philosophy was "an earnestness growing empty of all content".

None of the things I have said here will come as any surprise to observers of the contemporary philosophical scene. And it may well occur to such observers to wonder where all this is leading. Of course in reality no one can predict the future of philosophy. It is possible that the philosophical act may at some point recover its old authority by drawing on unknown resources whose nature we cannot begin to guess. The likelihood of this event is increased by the fact that, by its very nature, the philosophical act is not *public* nor the private preserve of those with special expertise; whence it follows that any changes to come would not necessarily be reflected in the technical literature on the subject. Of course even though we may know next to nothing about the immediate future, those of us who have faith and take seriously the message communicated by apocalyptic prophecy, may well "know" somewhat more about the *final* span of history, the end of time, that epoch at which, despite the fact that it is undatable, the arrow of each present moment is aimed, and which thus cannot be regarded as wholly unknown to us. Yet if we consult this apocalyptic prophecy, we find that it speaks of political power, of economics and trade, of propaganda; but it does not say a word about the wisdom of this world, about philosophy. It might not, in fact, come as such a great surprise if, in the Last Days, when the world is dominated by sophistry and a corrupt pseudophilosophy, true philosophy should be restored to its primal unity with theology and, as a result, disappear as a distinct and autonomous entity. This restoration of the primordial unity of the philosophical and theological interpretations of reality would not assume the naive form it possessed at the dawn of history, but rather would represent a painful, conscious reflection born of necessity. In other words, it might well be that at the end of history the only people who will examine and ponder the root of all things and the ultimate meaning of existence—i.e., the specific object of philosophical speculation—will be those who see with the eyes of *faith*.

The Reality of the Holy

54

Not Words but Reality

Recently a detailed and highly laudatory profile of a young metropolitan pastor appeared on television. This clergyman had abruptly transferred the celebration of Sunday religious services to the clubhouse where the young people of his parish used to meet and sit around drinking Coca-Cola and eating french fries. "If you won't come to hear me preach, why shouldn't I come to sit at your table and talk with you here?"

At first glance the behavior of this clergyman appears quite sensible, even natural. Of course it is not entirely clear whether this resolute man believed that by simply sitting and talking with people he could achieve everything which a Christian religious service is intended to achieve, or, if not everything, at least the most important thing, the essential purpose. Clearly the television commentators thought he did.

But regardless of the minister's opinion on this point, he was of course right in *one* respect: he abided by the ancient truth that anyone who wants to teach must find someone who will listen, and must, whether he likes it or not, seek out such people wherever they may happen to be—at a discothèque, having their evening pint at a bar, on the city streets, or sitting in front of a television screen.

Socrates practiced this same rule of thumb at the agora in Athens, just as the Apostle Paul did a few centuries later. If

Problems of Modern Faith, pp. 265–76, translated by Jan van Heurck. © 1985 Franciscan Herald Press, Chicago. Reprinted with permission.

Christian faith results from hearing the Word, then obviously the first order of business is to find some way to get the message across. After all, the word "gospel" means "good news" or "glad tidings", and a messenger responsible for spreading the news does not wait at home for someone to come to him. Instead he takes to the road and talks to people.

Thus the first step, always, is to preach the Gospel. This truism, which Christians have often ignored and at other times have blown up to almost mythic proportions and treated as the ultimate wisdom, was confirmed, a few short years ago, by the Second Vatican Council. However, at the same time the Council placed it in its proper perspective.

Clearly there is, in principle, no place where it would be inappropriate to preach the Gospel. The only criterion is that it be preached everywhere where there are people, for it is for people that it is intended. And naturally there is no reason whatever why, in order to preach the Gospel, one should not make use of all the available techniques of communication.

However, we must also consider the other side of the coin. Of course the initial task is speaking and preaching, and this preliminary task must be performed over and over again. Nevertheless, talking cannot be the essential element in divine worship. By its very nature, speech points toward something which is not speech. What is it then? It's reality! A friend of mine used to declaim on this subject, repeating the same dictum over and over in an emphatic tone, like the refrain of a song. (And by the way, I heartily concur with his views!) He used to say: "I do not go to church to hear someone talk or listen to a sermon; I go to church because something *happens* there." Naturally, in a matter of such importance, the personal views of my friend, myself or any other individual do not matter in the least. In my opinion the only thing that matters is what the Church itself, the *kyriaké* or sacred community which "belongs to the Lord", has believed and thought and said about this subject down through the centuries. And from its very inception the Church, like my friend, has said that the

core of religious worship is in fact an *event,* i.e., something indeed "happens".

And what is it that happens? I, as a layman—neither a priest
nor a theologian—would like to try to spell out in, so to speak,
the most primitive terms, the answer to this question—an answer which, once again, is that of the Church itself. For indeed, in our times it seems necessary to spell out *all* fundamental facts in the most elementary terms.

Moreover, I will be speaking as a believer, as a Roman
Catholic Christian; and probably only another believer will
agree with what I say. Nevertheless I think that even the unbeliever may be expected to at least be aware of how a believer
interprets the matters in question, just as I would doubtless be
interested to learn, let us say, how an orthodox Hindu interprets the fundamental doctrines of Hinduism.

To avoid misinterpreting everything about Christian religious ceremonial, the first thing one must understand about it
is its derivative, subordinate and secondary character. What
takes place in the rite is essentially an echo or reminiscence, a
continuation. Or more precisely, it is, in a quite specific sense
which I will define later, the rendering present, the becoming
present, of an event which occurred in the remote past:
namely, that event which we customarily designate by the
theological term "Incarnation". Consequently, anyone who is
unable to accept the earlier, primordial event, whose priority
is both of time and of essence, as something which *really happened,* will never be able to understand or "realize", either in
thought or in action, what "happens" during the liturgical
worship of the Church.

But that primordial event which is described as having occurred "in the fullness of time" and which in fact constitutes
the central event of human history, is not merely difficult to
comprehend but is downright incredible. It is something
whose truth I would never accept on the testimony of even the
most reliable chronicler or the most inspired philosopher or
theologian, if I did not know that it was authenticated by what

Plato calls a *theios logos,* a divine word or word of God—i.e., by revelation in the most literal sense of the term. The event in question is in fact an impossible one—or so, at least, one is tempted to think if one is not secretly aware that absolute consummation, fulfillment or perfection *always* appears to us unprecedented, a thing which we would never have expected to occur. "Ever impossible seems the rose", Goethe says in one of his poems. As you can see, I am truly speaking as a layman, for of course the incomprehensibility of the rose as it reveals itself in the act of blooming is as nothing compared to the glory of that event we are now discussing, which totally transcends man's powers of imagination: that event in which God himself becomes a man and, as the New Testament says, in an image drawn from the language of pastoral nomads, pitches his tent among us.

And yet this rounding out of the circle in which the beginning and the end, the primal Origin of the creation and the ultimate Consummation of the creative process, meet and touch in Christ; this closing of the ring does not constitute the whole of the event rendered present in divine worship. The idea of such a harmonious circle appeals to our minds, which by nature desire a unified "system". However, the belief that the harmony constitutes the whole could easily tempt us into an erroneous, unhistorical-Gnostic misinterpretation of God's Incarnation.

For the truth is that the essential element of this event is such that it must necessarily shatter any harmonious formula we construct about the universe. The essential element is the fact that at a datable moment within historical time ("under Pontius Pilate"), this God who became a man in Jesus Christ, performed an act of self-surrender and allowed himself to be killed by men, by his own people, in order to make it possible for these same men to share in the life of God.

We will never understand why such a ghastly sacrificial death on the public pillory of shame was necessary to achieve this—although, on the other hand, many of us have personally experienced the truth that no man has greater love than this, that he should lay down his life for his friends.

Let me repeat once again that anyone who, for whatever reasons, does not accept the historical reality of this primordial event—the Incarnation of God and the sacrificial death of Jesus Christ—must inevitably fail to understand the mystery celebrated in Christian worship. For as I have stated, what "happens" in the liturgical worship of the Church derives from that primordial event. It is by nature a secondary phenomenon.

However, this assertion can easily lead to misunderstandings. Above all, it does *not* imply that Christian divine worship is merely a kind of commemorative ceremony designed to perform the perfectly natural and even meaningful task of celebrating and preserving the memory of something which happened in the past.

At this point I would like to say something in defense of an idea which the great rationalist philosophers of the eighteenth and nineteenth centuries repeatedly employed as an argument against Christianity. To be sure, essentially this idea is completely false; but nevertheless, one should be able to understand its underlying point. I am referring to an argument against Christianity which has been expressed in a variety of terms by Kant, Lessing and many other thinkers from the eighteenth century down to the present day: Why should a person find it necessary to base his life on a historical event which took place at some time in the past, and indeed, is it even permissible for him to do so? Of course, these thinkers reasoned, one can accept a faith based on necessary, compelling truth; this presents no problem. But can one expect a man with a critical mind to accept a "historical faith" (as Kant calls it) which derives its authority from an event in the remote past that necessarily involved many contingent or fortuitous factors? There are many ways in which one might respond to this question. One way would be to counter it with the question of whether absolutely necessary certainties can exist for any mind which is not likewise absolute. All the same, *one* aspect of this objection to the Christian faith is quite correct. If the divine Logos actually became a man and revealed itself in Christ, then it is in fact impossible to regard this event as confined to the time span of a few brief years at the beginning of our era, which lies almost twenty centuries in the past. If God really became incarnate, and if his Incarnation can with justice compel man to change his life, then we have no alternative but to conceive of this Incarnation as something which is *still present* and which will *remain present* for all future time. To be sure, the Incarnation does not endure as a "necessary truth of reason" in Lessing's sense of the term. Instead its presence is that of a physical event which, although it is incomprehensible and can be grasped only by the believer, is in fact absolutely real.

It is precisely this clearly perceptible presence of the Incarnation and the sacrificial death of Christ which lies at the heart of the celebration of the Christian mystery of the Eucharist. This presence is the reality experienced by those who take part in the celebration.

"That's all well and good" (one might say at this point), "but after all, all the visible, perceptible events which take place during the liturgical celebration are merely symbolic." *No,* I would answer, not "*merely* symbolic". But *sacramental!* To be sure, a sacrament belongs to the same class as a sign or a symbol, but it is not "*merely* symbolic". It not only *signifies* something but, like no other sign in the world, it at the same time *effectuates* what it means. In other words, it creates objective, solid reality. Naturally it does not do so through a purely nonverbal, "magical" act. The spoken word is not irrelevant here; language plays a part. Nevertheless, the assertion of a famous modern theologian that the essence of the sacrament resides in the word is highly debatable and can easily lead one astray. No, the decisive and distinctive mark of the sacramental word is the fact that when it is spoken, the thing of which it speaks actually occurs!

What happens in the liturgical celebration of the Eucharist is something for which all the religions of mankind have expressed longing, dimly sensed was coming, and as a rule even prefigured—namely, the actual presence of God among men, or more precisely, the physical presence of the divine Logos made man, and the presence of his sacrificial death, in the midst of the congregation celebrating the mysteries. Those "celebrating" the mysteries! This very fact of "celebration" makes it clear that the event in question cannot take place just anywhere, and that those who take part cannot behave in any way they choose. Events of such dignity and majesty simply cannot take place everywhere or anywhere one likes, nor can they take place before any crowd of indifferent people who happen to be there. The enactment of such rites requires a space which has been expressly segregated from the trivial and everyday. This is true even if, as has often been the case in the concentration camps of despotic regimes, the boundary wall is formed solely by the living bodies of the celebrants themselves. The prime requirement of worship is this community of faithful worshippers.

Normally (that is, apart from emergency conditions, which we are not discussing at the moment) an *altar* is also a necessity of worship. Since the time of St. Augustine, the "sacrament of the altar" has been the accepted term for the Christian celebration of the Eucharist. In its interior, invisible essence an altar is not merely a table, a piece of furniture, but at the same time is also the altar stone on which the sacrifice is made. Of course, as the "Lord's table", the Christian altar is also essentially the locus of a communal, ritual meal.

This brings us a new aspect of our theme, namely, the question of how the Christian shares, as he is expressly intended to do, in what objectively and really "happens" in the celebration of the Eucharist. In other words, how does he share in what happens beyond all human speech, preaching and prayer, and behind the symbolic action?

How, in fact, do I participate, how do I really share in any event? Do I do so merely by being present when it takes place? Obviously not! Is mere observation enough, regardless of how attentive and intense my observation may be? How, in this special and totally exceptional case, does that event occur which we designate by the word "communication" (a term which, incidentally, has now degenerated into something of a vogue word)? Obviously the word "communication" is closely related to "communion" and "communicate", which at one time, in Christian usage, unequivocally and almost exclusively designated that very participation and sharing whose nature we are at the moment attempting to plumb. Recently the word "communicate", which derived from the technical jargon of sociology and lost some of its precision and specificity in the transfer, has become part of the everyday vocabulary of the average educated man. Such shifts in the meanings of words offer us the opportunity to do something which, quite apart from the intrinsic importance of words themselves, appears advisable or even essential from time to time: the opportunity to examine something which has become overly familiar from the standpoint of the uninitiate, the man who does "not yet belong", and thus to perceive its original meaning with fresh eyes, with the eyes, as it were, of a stranger who is seeking it for the first time.

This is exactly what happened to me when I read the remarkable book by the French journalist André Frossard, *Dieu existe, je l'ai rencontré*. This book remained on the international bestseller lists for a long time, for which reason I almost neglected to so much as glance at it.

Frossard's book is a magnificent account, by a formerly average, secular-minded, modern intellectual, of an experience which might more or less justifiably be termed "mystical"—an account, moreover, which, because of its simplicity and lack of pretension, carries real conviction. Most significantly, the author describes the aftermath of his mystical experience, his reactions to his reasonably systematic attempt to study Christian doctrine as interpreted by the Roman Catholic Church. In the past he had known the teachings of the Church, if at all, only through hearsay; but now he greeted each fresh discovery with enthusiasm. Each doctrine he studied appeared like a well-aimed shot which hit the center of the target—except for one! One thing overwhelmed him with a delighted astonishment and wonder: the doctrine of which we have been speaking, namely, man's participation in the Godhead made present in the sacrament of the Eucharist: "Of all the gifts which Christianity had spread out before me, the most beautiful was this: that Divine Love should have found this unique way to communicate itself, in bread, in the food of the poor!"

Here, from this new vantage point, we can look back at the question which we asked at the beginning of this essay. The decisive and essential thing which "happens" in the Christian celebration of the Eucharist is not talk and not preaching, but that *event,* that *reality* of which those who preach the word of God can, at best, merely speak. This reality is that (in the absolute sense of the word) extraordinary event, distinct from the realities of normal, everyday life, in which the sacrifice of Christ is brought into the present moment so that Christ himself, really present in the sacred bread of the Host, is united with the faithful celebrants in their common feast.

Because of what I should choose to call their arrogant spiritualism, people who think primarily in abstract, conceptual terms are particularly prone to regard the tangible, concrete act of feeding on God himself and sharing a meal with him as materialistic or even primitive. In my student days, I actually heard a sociology professor refer to the Lord's Supper as a "Negroid atavism". And even a man of St. Augustine's spiritual stature appears to be defending himself against some intellectual temptation, to which he himself is threatening to succumb, when he vehemently insists that the sacrament of the Eucharist does *not* represent a "verbal event" ("Not language, not letters, not resonant sound"), but instead involves the Body of the Lord, incarnate in the matter formed from the fruits of earth.

However, this thing, the Eucharist, whose nature may appear dubious or insufficiently "spiritual" to a man sitting unmolested at his desk, has, again and again, for many thousands of people living in the most desperate conditions and facing the ultimate problems of existence, proved a source of true comfort and healing, and above all has proved to be the only tangible reality in their lives, the only solid ground beneath their feet. It has proved so for the prisoners under totalitarian regimes, for the doomed and the dying, who were beyond the reach of any human exhortation, human words, human talk; who could communicate only with the reality of God—in the Sacrament of Bread.

55

"Sacred Action"

What is a "sacred action"? I think that it would be difficult to find anyone in the civilized Western world who had no notion of what a liturgical religious service was like, i.e., who was wholly ignorant of what the Second Vatican Council calls "a preeminently 'sacred action' ", *actio sacra praecellenter*. For ex-

Problems of Modern Faith, pp. 24–29, translated by Jan van Heurck. © 1985 Franciscan Herald Press, Chicago. Reprinted with permission.

ample, everyone is aware that a "sacred action" is not simply carried out, executed or "wound up", but rather is "celebrated". Recently it was proven that the word *celebrate* has meant the same thing "from the earliest days of classical Roman antiquity until its absorption into Christian liturgical language": namely, the performance of an action by the community in a manner distinct from that employed in carrying out its everyday affairs. Moreover, a "sacred action", as distinct from a purely interior act such as prayer, the love of God, or faith, represents a social act, a *physical* event represented in visible forms, in the audible language of homily and instruction, in bodily action and symbolic gesture, in the special character of the vestments and vessels, in preaching and song, and even in shared silence—an event in which the observer or "reader" of this spectacle or language performs an act analogous to the act performed by the priest, and indeed helps the priest to celebrate his act.

Of course a serious, thoughtful observer who attends, let us say, a solemn High Mass at the Abbey of Maria Laach, may wonder whether this undeniably impressive event actually represents anything more than a mystery play performed with a high degree of artistry, a magnificently staged religious drama which, however, at bottom is nothing but a spectacle, an empty ceremony, pure "theater". Strangely enough, Thomas Aquinas formulated a similar objection to the view which he himself actually held, when he questioned whether the theatrical element of symbolic actions might not be incompatible with the "authenticity" of the religious rite. His reply was that in fact religious worship had something in common with poetry in that both depicted, through images accessible to the senses, things which could not be directly grasped by the reason *(ratio)*. However, naturally when a modern man raises this objection, he means something entirely different by it than St. Thomas did: He is not asking about the "meaning" of the sacred action, but about its truth content. To put it mildly, he questions whether anything solid, tangible and real takes place in the course of the action; he disputes the fact that something on the order of the divine presence is actually manifested in its performance. In other words, he denies its *sacramental* character. The question he poses is in fact the crucial question on whose answer everything depends.

Naturally our reply to the question of whether a particular event, which we can experience through our senses, possesses the quality of a sacrament; whether there is in fact any such thing as a sacrament; and if so, exactly what it is will depend on the kind and quality of our faith. Yet perhaps even the unbeliever may be expected to take note of the Christian—or perhaps in this case one would have to say, of the Roman Catholic—interpretation of a sacrament. The Roman Catholic view is that in this particular, unique case—the case of the sacrament—the "symbols" manifest in physical action and in the audible spoken word do not simply *mean* something, but that during their enactment that thing which they *mean*—purification, the eradication of guilt, the consumption of the true Body of the Lord—becomes an objective *reality*. Moreover, it does so not by virtue of the power possessed by those human beings who perform the rite, and certainly not through the power of the concrete symbols themselves, but through the power of God, which is in reality the sole effectual force operative in the sacramental rite. (I can already hear someone raising the old hue and cry: "Magical thinking!"But I would prefer to return to the subject of magic a little later.)

Before proceeding I must clear up another foggy issue. Admittedly the very notion of a "sacrament" is an awesome and overwhelming thing, and one cannot try to persuade anyone to accept its validity. Yet one thing must be made absolutely clear: if a sacred action, above all the Christian celebration of the Eucharist, does *not* constitute a sacrament in the sense I have described—in other words, if the divine presence does not really manifest itself, in a special and exceptional way, in the performance of this action—then in fact all discussion of the sacred would be, at bottom, without foundation. In this case all manifestations of the sacred, especially its liturgical and ritual manifestations, would represent nothing more than a bit of pious folklore—perhaps worthy of our respect, perhaps worthy of preservation on aesthetic grounds, but lacking any tangible reality—and could therefore, with justice, be sacrificed to the harsh depredations of history and its relentless "Forward march!" Moreover, I am convinced that the ultimate intellectual root of all the programmatic advocacy of "desacralization"—particularly when this "desacralization" is propounded on "theological" grounds—is nothing other than the denial of sacramentality. In other words, its root is the belief that what we still refer to as a "sacred action" is in reality a mere "show" put on by human beings, and that, viewed from an objective and "impartial" standpoint, *absolutely nothing happens* during this show, least of all the manifestation of the real presence of the divine. The inevitable consequence of this reasoning is clearly apparent. Not only does it become senseless to regard the church (as a building) as anything but what Harvey Cox called a human space, but also there no longer exists the slightest reason for regarding the priest as a "consecrated" person, as a person dedicated to the sacred. And it would be difficult to persuade me that the most profound and perhaps even the sole cause of the "modern crisis over the image of the priest", which has given rise to so much discussion, is not, once again, the refusal or inability (an inability determined by a multiplicity of factors) to recognize and accept the relationship between the sacramental, consecratory act of the priest and the manifestation of God's presence in the mystery of the Eucharistic sacrifice. This refusal in turn inevitably results in the need to "redefine" the distinctive function of the priest, to analyze his specific task in terms of something other than the performance of the sacramental rite: for example, in terms of the "service of the Word", of the

"meditation on the Word", the "unification of the parish", social work or even in terms of revolution.

On the other hand, anyone who is convinced that in the performance of the sacred action, or more precisely in the celebration of the Eucharist—dimly foreseen, longed for, and prefigured in all the religions of mankind—something totally
exceptional, something which is, in an absolute sense, out of
the ordinary, actually takes place: namely, God's physical
presence among men—takes for granted the existence of a
boundary shutting out the region of everyday life, and considers it natural that this boundary should make its existence felt
with particular clarity and power. *Rapi,* to be seized and carried away from the Here and Now—this, as the Church itself
has stated, is what it means for man to be in the presence of
God. This concept of rapture is not a derogation of life in this
world. We are asked neither to ignore nor to forget this life.
But we *are* supposed to walk through it and to climb above it.
Moreover, in a sense what the Greek Fathers said about religious feast days also applies to the sacred action: It takes place
"neither in this aeon nor upon the earth". In any case, the sacred action provides a tangible foretaste and beginning of the
life of beatitude which ultimately awaits us at God's table, a
true *inchoatio vitae aeternae* ("incipience of eternal life").

And regardless of whether the members of a religious congregation regard themselves as a *parochia* (from the Greek
paroikia), "a group of strangers or sojourners" [whence our
word "parish"], or whether they consider themselves the citizens of the coming Kingdom, they draw a boundary line between themselves and the normal, everyday way of life, as it
is lived by the citizens of an ordinary community. They may
celebrate their liturgy in a makeshift church in the suburbs; in
the dancehall of a village where the Diaspora has driven them
into exile; in a cathedral whose costly hall is filled with
stained-glass windows symbolizing the Heavenly Jerusalem;

or in a concentration camp where, for a few minutes, a living wall of bodies creates a makeshift sanctuary and screens it from the grip of the executioners. All these places have *one* thing in common: they stand out, by their poverty as much as by their splendor and prodigality, from the dwelling places of everyday existence, from their deathly penury as well as from their deceitful luxury and comfort.

And nothing seems more natural to a man, when he is inside such an enclosure, than to behave "differently" than he behaves in other places such as a sports arena or a place of business. Naturally, in this sequestered place one continues to speak a human language, and yet it is a "different" language—different in character, in intonation, in vocabulary, in gesture.

56

The Grandeur and Misery of Man

The phenomenon of "desacralization"—regardless of whether one views it as a historical process which happens to be taking place, or advocates it as a principle—involves not only theological but philosophical, or more precisely, anthropological "heresies" as well.

For example, anyone who fails to realize that there is nothing in man's nature which is "purely spiritual", but that there is nothing that is "purely physical" either, will in all likelihood

Problems of Modern Faith, pp. 36–39, translated by Jan van Heurck. © 1985 Franciscan Herald Press, Chicago. Reprinted with permission.

be incapable of appreciating or meaningfully enacting that "structure of forms visible and perceptible to the senses" which we call a sacred action. Romano Guardini is correct in his assertion that the ancient philosophical proposition *anima forma corporis* ("The soul is the form of the body"), which Christians have repeatedly tended to forget or even to proscribe, but which is reconfirmed every day by the empirical exploration of the real and living human being, is basic to all liturgical culture. This proposition is in fact a kind of password, the knowledge of which determines whether one is admitted to or barred from the world of the sacred.

For example, it is only in terms of this proposition that one can understand the fixed and predetermined form of sacred "language", the language of gesture, symbol and word. This fixed character is not determined solely by the communal nature of the sacred action—even though it is quite true that free improvisation, as a response to the inspiration of the moment, is possible only to the individual. The fixed quality of liturgy may be more closely linked to that same principle of excluding the random or capricious which bars us from arbitrarily altering a poem once it has achieved its finished form.

Naturally the bipartite truth, *anima forma corporis*, is subject to attack on two fronts. Its validity may be disputed either by dedicated "spiritualists" or by their opposite numbers, the proponents of what one could call "corporealism". In the first case, the spiritual act is regarded as the only decisive factor in worship, and thus the manner in which it is expressed is considered purely a matter of "externals" and hence a matter of indifference. In the second case, although for completely different reasons, the same claim is made that the form of the language employed in the rite is entirely optional. Prefabricated forms of worship are regarded as unwarranted constraint, and even singing in unison is felt to be a form of "manipulation". Instead of following the established ritual, we are told that it would be more "natural" to swim with the current, to simply "let ourselves go". It is disquieting to note that, in effect, both these species of rejection of liturgical norms lead to virtually identical results. Neither the "spiritualist" nor the "corporealist" thesis acknowledges the unique opportunity offered the individual by the challenge to transcend the limitations of the self *precisely by* submitting to the objectivity of consummate form.

Above all, anyone who disputes the truth of the proposition *anima forma corporis* will inevitably fail to grasp a concept fundamental to the understanding of the sacred: he will never comprehend what is meant by a *symbol.* He will never understand the fact that it is completely natural for a human being not to act exclusively with a view to achieving certain ends, but also, from time to time, to create a sign, even if this sign consists in nothing more than lighting a candle; lighting it *not* in order to light up a room, but to express the heightened solemnity or festivity of the occasion, to express adoration and thanks, or to commemorate a dead person whom one loved.

The deliberately "non-utilitarian" character of such a sign calls to mind another element of symbolic action: the element of excess and superabundance, the absence of calculation, the almost wasteful prodigality. The first mouthful of wine from the jug is not "used", is not drunk, but is "wasted" and poured into the sea or onto the flagstones as a gift to the gods. Quite deliberately, people do not build a purely functional place of assembly, but instead build a cathedral or the church of Ronchamp. And naturally the bells of Notre Dame were never really intended to serve the purpose of announcing the time or transmitting information. At least this was not their primary purpose, for if it had been, the invention of the wristwatch would have rendered them obsolete. No, these bells always were and still are a nonverbal form of rejoicing. They represent abundance and waste.

But what about the counterargument stressing the value of simplicity and even of poverty? Isn't it right too? I do not hesitate for a moment to say: yes, naturally it is right to emphasize the importance of simplicity and poverty. However, I do not believe that any overarching synthesis which attempts to embrace both meagerness and pomp can ever smooth over the discord between them and lead to total harmony. For the tension between them simply cannot be denied. Josef Andreas Jungmann lists this tension as one of the seven or eight antitheses inseparable from the act of divine worship. Song cannot be "thrifty" and still remain song. On the other hand, the manifestation of splendor is not necessarily the same thing as material display (although of course it does not rule it out). In any case, in no sense does the extravagance we are speaking of here imply the display of money and possessions. It is the spontaneous manifestation of personal, interior riches, of that wealth which consists in the experience of the actual presence of God among men. Thus once again we have reached the core of the sacred, that element without which everything we call "sacred" is bound to remain mere routine, a brief and fitful response, without which it will, in fact, remain mere "theater", a "show" which, although it may still be impressive, at bottom lacks all reality. This core is the presence of God.

However, at the same time that we behold this image of abundance, we must confront the image of the most radical human poverty, not material but existential want. We would be desolate if we had to live in a world containing only things which we could dispose of and use, but nothing which we could simply enjoy, without thought of any utilitarian end; a world in which there was specialized expertise, but no philosophical reflection on life as a whole; a world in which there was investigation but no memory; diversion and the pleasant pastimes of the workaday world, but no true holidays, no great poetry or music. If this is true, then how much more desperate would our situation be if we were to be walled up alive inside a desacralized, totally "worldly world" where we were never granted the opportunity, at least now and then, to rise above the here and now, the historical realities of the moment, and to enter that vaster realm of existence which we were likewise intended to inhabit: to enter it not merely through the mode of philosophical reflection and not merely through the catharsis of art, but *in reality,* in the living of life itself, and first and foremost in the sacred action?

"Finis" Means Both End and Goal

57

Future without a Past and Hope
with No Foundation?

It is obvious to anyone who has even a nodding acquaintance
with the writings of contemporary theologians and anthropologists that they attribute a unique significance to the concepts of "hope" and "the future". One finds repeated over and
over the key terms coined by Ernst Bloch, "Utopia", "front",
"novum" ("novelty"). One hears of the "primacy of the
future". Christianity is termed "the religion of the absolute
future". Christians are said to be "quite simply those 'who
have hope' ". And the multifarious elements of theology are
being reduced to one single element, that of eschatology.

I myself have, to some degree, participated in the creation
of this intellectual and terminological vogue. For example, I
too have spoken of the future as the only thing which really
belongs to us, and have said that hope represents man's authentic response to the reality of that part of his existence
which has not yet come into being. I am recalling this fact for
a reason; for in the contribution which I am about to make to
this debate, I shall, willy-nilly, be compelled to defend a position contrary to that I expressed in the statements just cited.

For I am in fact convinced that all this talk about the "not-
yet", about the future, about hope and eschatology, reflects an
overemphasis on some aspects of life at the expense of others,

Problems of Modern Faith, pp. 157–72, translated by Jan van Heurck. © 1985
Franciscan Herald Press, Chicago. Reprinted with permission.

and that at the very least we need to set about filling in the rest of the picture, if not to revise it altogether. At a certain point, I believe it becomes a mistake to place such emphasis on the future, on eschatology. In saying this I am thinking less of the original authors of the concepts in question than I am of the frequently oversimplified terminology employed in public debate of the issues. However, this terminology derives its authority from the aforementioned authors, and thus they may not be entirely exempt from responsibility for its usage, despite the fact that their views may frequently be misrepresented.

To my mind there can be no question of regarding as mere "misrepresentation" the relationship between the new theology of hope and the future and the shocking interpretation of this theology expounded by the Marxist Roger Garaudy, who regards the new approach as the result of reflection by Christians on the true essence of the Christian faith, and expresses his warm approval. Obviously, Garaudy says, in terms of the new Christian theology, man's "existence" now consists in "being liberated from his nature and his past *(être libéré de sa nature et de son passé)* through the divine grace revealed in Christ, liberated for a life of free choices". In my view the really noteworthy feature of this assertion is the fact that it does *not* reflect a misunderstanding or misinterpretation of the theological views in question, but that, on the contrary, it takes these views at their word, thus revealing hidden consequences and implications which their authors probably never had in mind when they conceived them, but which nevertheless cannot be adjudged inconsistent with their theories. It is for this reason that I call Garaudy's interpretation shocking or frightening. At least I know that *I* would be deeply dismayed if I were a Christian theologian who found himself being "interpreted" in such a manner. Of course one's reaction to Garaudy's statement will depend on what, precisely, one understands by man's "nature" and his "past".

In fact it will be necessary to define all our terms with greater precision. My own position and the criticisms and

counterquestions which it provokes must be formulated with
equal care. So: *Is* human existence in fact exclusively oriented
toward that which has not yet come to pass? Above all, does
"Christian faith" signify nothing more than "trust in the
future"? Garaudy's interpretation of this question — which, it
should be noted, he once again claims is based on the conclusions arrived at by Christian theologians themselves in the
course of reflecting on their faith — reads as follows: "Hence-
forth, to believe means to be completely open to the future"
(Croire, c'est désormais être entièrement ouvert à l'avenir). (Incidentally, as you may have noticed, this statement is an almost
word-for-word quotation of Rudolf Bultmann's statement:
"For that is precisely the meaning of 'faith': to open oneself
freely to the future.") But doesn't Christian faith also imply,
in addition to this openness toward the future, the acceptance,
as true and real, of something which has already happened in
the past — something which is *not*, in any sense, confined to the
past, but which nevertheless did occur at some past moment
of historical time, which since that time has continued to
elapse? Have we, in short, characterized the existential situation of man and of the Christian adequately or completely if
we describe it as the situation of one who hopes? Anyone who
raises criticisms or questions of this kind is liable to be accused
of advocating the same traditional, archaic position which is
attacked in modern anthropological and theological polemics,
the very position which, so to speak, made this attack necessary in the first place. But of course my reflections are not intended to advocate any such position. Clearly I do not side
with those who champion what Ernst Bloch calls a "purely
static concept of being" and an extrahistorical view of the
world and existence. To be sure, the matter becomes more
complex if one attempts to establish the identity of these
tradition-minded opponents of the new views. For which
thinkers, specifically, can really be considered representative
of this fundamentally "undynamic" school of thought? Probably one would be justified in including among them the

proponents of any academic metaphysics which bears the rationalistic stamp of the Enlightenment, as well as exponents of that pseudoscholasticism which derives its character more from Christian Wolff than from Thomas Aquinas. However, Thomas himself, and the other great Doctors of Western Christendom, do *not* by any means fall into this category. I regard it as a matter of some importance to say this because, if I am not mistaken, those modern thinkers who talk so much about the future, hope, and eschatology are in part attacking these great Doctors, and perhaps even regard them as their principal targets.

In reality Thomas Aquinas, who may in a sense be considered representative of scholasticism and Western tradition in general, regarded as the hallmark of created existence the fact that created beings were always "on the way" toward something, so that existence possessed the structure of a journey, a dynamic orientation toward the future. Of course, clearly he also strongly emphasizes the role of the *past* in created existence.

For whenever a person is convinced that some prior event or fact shapes or helps to shape human existence, including man's present and future, *memoria*, i.e., a recollection which renders the past present, plays a legitimate and necessary role in his thought. In other words, given the presupposition that the present is influenced by the past, looking back to the beginnings of things, the deliberate effort not to forget but to remember, and thus to preserve, the past, represents one of the indispensable, fundamental acts of intellectual life which alone makes possible any meaningful future.

But that *a priori* factor, that datum prior to all others, which most decisively affects our existence, is *we ourselves,* i.e., that which we are by virtue of our created state. In other words, the first given, that which preexists all else and makes our existence what it is, is our own human "nature". As we all know, for the theologian, the word "nature" has acquired a somewhat dubious ring, or at least a dubious overtone. Nevertheless, there exists a current in Western thought, extending from St. Augustine to, let us say, Immanuel Kant, in which the meaning of the phrase "by nature" is identical to that of "by virtue of the created state". But this datum which exists by nature and by virtue of the created state, this factor which proceeded from the creative plan of God and his power to confer existence—in other words the nature of man as a created being, as well as the nature of all things—represents their irrevocable origin and precondition of all that we ourselves are capable of achieving, as well as of every additional endowment which God may bestow upon us. Thus whenever, in a given situation, we choose and attempt to realize the good, our actions—despite the fact that, as is only natural, our eyes remain fixed on the future—do not represent something totally unprecedented and pristine which has no roots in the past. Instead we are continuing something which began long ago, something primordial which—without our active participation and perhaps even *in opposition to* our conscious will —has always existed, and is continuing to operate, in the innermost core of our "nature", of the essence with which we were endowed at our creation. We are hearkening to a voice which speaks within us by nature, but which is at the same time our own voice, the voice of *our* primordial conscience; and we are following the specifications of a primal blueprint which we not only did not design ourselves, but which we only come to know little by little, and perhaps never learn to know completely. And even the "newness of life" which we call "grace" and which, as believing Christians, we are convinced is imparted to us, or at least has become accessible to us, through Christ—even this unmerited gift presupposes as, so to speak, its "point of departure", that which we are and possess and are capable of doing, by virtue of our created state. Moreover, this and nothing else is the true meaning of a proposition which has been misinterpreted a thousand times:

gratia supponit naturam ("Grace builds on nature"); or in other words, "That which exists by nature always comes first."

However, we do not learn to know this "first"—our human nature and the divine design which informs it—as if we were discovering, by progressively amassing greater experience of the world, something which was hitherto completely unknown to us or which only comes into being gradually over the passage of time. Instead, if we come to know it at all, we know it in the manner of someone who, as it were, closes his eyes in order to remember something which has always been there, which he has always possessed and which, for a long time, he has actually known, but which always was and remains in danger of being forgotten. Quite properly, people use the word "memento" ("remember") to describe phenomena of this kind: "Remember . . . remember something which, deep down, you have always known" (*memento homo quia pulvis es,* "Remember, man, that thou art dust!"). This, moreover, is precisely what is implied by Plato's doctrine of *anamnesis* or "recollection", as the act in which we glimpse the "Ideas", the "essences" of the soul, the state or virtue. And Ernst Bloch is quite correct when he says that the Socratic-Platonic cognition of "essence" simply involves an "*after-thought*", an *ex post facto* reflection or retrospection; but this fact does not constitute an argument against Plato. After all, we ourselves do not invent or think up that which truly exists, including our own nature. Instead we *encounter* it, as well as our knowledge of it, as something preexistent, as a prior datum. As for Bloch's other critical comment on Plato's theory of *anamnesis*—i.e., the fact that this theory regards being, and above all essence, as something confined to the past—this is nothing more than a play on words and must be classed among those brilliant but fallacious conclusions in which the works of this author abound. For despite the fact that the "essence" of the world and of man can never, in ultimate terms, be grasped or defined by the finite intellect, nevertheless this essence, preconceived in the divine creative plan, is by its very nature *not* "passé". On the contrary, despite the fact that it has existed "always" and "from the beginning", it still is today, and will be throughout the future, the entelechy which fuels the dynamics of material existence and at the same time defines its interior norms. It is both the pattern after which existence is modelled and the image of the goal toward which it tends.

Thus—to state my first thesis—to the degree that, as anthropologists, we presuppose and examine the substance of what is truly human; or, as theologians, we take seriously the idea that man and the world possess a specific character, a "nature", with which they were endowed at their creation—to that degree we are not dealing exclusively or even primarily with the future. Given these assumptions, it becomes impossible for us to conceive of man as liberated "from his nature and his past", as Roger Garaudy puts it. Indeed, we cannot regard such a "liberation" as either meaningful or desirable. This notion of liberation would imply a view or an ideal of man as a being who was not designed and summoned into existence by God, but who, on the contrary, designs and invents and creates himself. Clearly such a view would place us squarely in the camp of that nihilistic Existentialism whose basic principle was formulated with great precision by Jean-Paul Sartre. *Il n'y a pas de nature humaine, puisqu'il n'y a pas de Dieu pour la concevoir,* or "There is no such thing as human nature because there is no God to have designed it."

My second thesis relates to the concept of "tradition", or more precisely to the concept of "*sacred* tradition". The thesis is this: anyone who regards the reality underlying the concept of "sacred tradition" as something which decisively influences the existence of man in history must by definition look toward the past as well as the future—must look toward some earlier, antecedent event. For "sacred tradition" is the name we give to that process of transmission and reception in and through which the identity of a revelation (information, promise,

commandment) which was once imparted to man from a su-
prahuman source is preserved and kept alive in the present
over the course of many generations. By definition the concept of "tradition" implies that not everyone, not every individual, has personal, direct access to the *traditum* or *tradendum*,
to that which is "passed on" by way of tradition. In the case
of *sacred* tradition, this means that God has not spoken to everyone, but only to a "chosen" few—patriarchs, prophets,
apostles. And it is these "inspired" individuals, the original recipients of the word of God, who pass this word on to other
men. All these "other men"—above all those born long after
the revelatory event—partake in this divine utterance, this
pálai légetai ("what was said of old"), or more specifically, this
utterance of "God, who at sundry times and in divers manners
spake in time past" *(multifariam, multisque modis)* but "hath in
these last days spoken unto us by his Son" (Heb 1:1–2), only,
and yet quite genuinely, by establishing a link with its original
recipients, by listening to their words. Of course, strictly
speaking the "listening" and the "faith" of the "others" are
not directed toward the original recipients and witnesses of the
revelation, but solely toward the One who spoke to them in
time past. Thus each successive generation, representing as it
does the last link in the chain of tradition, has the responsibility to hear and understand the original message in the purest
possible mode, without omitting anything, and also without
adding anything which might distort its meaning. And so,
once again, those born after the revelatory event must necessarily look toward the past to find the divine message which
is prior to, and a given of, their existence.

This is especially true of theologians—insofar as theology
can be defined as *doctrina secundum revelationem divinam*
("teaching in accordance with divine revelation"), as the interpretation of revelation, i.e., as the attempt to make clear to
each new generation what was truly meant and said in the
word of God. Naturally this task is oriented toward the *future*,
for its purpose is to preserve the divine message for coming

generations and to maintain its presence in human society. Moreover, the future is justifiably a concern of Christian theology because the *content* of God's word possesses, to an eminent degree, the character of a *promise*. Thus in this respect I am in complete agreement with Jürgen Moltmann when he says: "Tradition is a sending forward into the novelty of the promised future" and "The Gospel, being a promise, is a pledge of the future envisaged in that promise." Nevertheless, I believe that the essential task of theology is not to articulate and formulate the ever-shifting dynamics of human existence, but simply to recall, proclaim, preserve from oblivion, maintain the identity of, and keep alive in the present moment, something preexistent: namely, the revelation, the word of God, which was spoken at some time in the past. To be sure, this task can be achieved only through an unceasing intellectual reassimilation, an ever fresh formulation and interpretation, of the revelation. But the thing which is actually to be interpreted preexists the interpreter as well as those to whom he addresses his findings. In the same way, Christian religious worship is clearly characterized by the fact that Christians are awaiting the culmination of this worship at some point in the future, namely in the coming of the Lord at the end of time (*donec veniat,* "till he come", 1 Cor 11:26); and yet at the same time divine worship is preeminently a memorial celebration in which is proclaimed the death of the Lord. And the Sacred Bread of the Host is indeed *cibus viatorum,* food for those on a journey, but also, and above all, it is *memoriale mortis Domini,* eaten in commemoration of the death of the Lord.

At this point I will attempt to formulate some tentative replies to certain criticisms or questions regarding my view of tradition, which Jürgen Moltmann addressed to me in his book *Theology of Hope.*

The first question relates to my resort to the Platonic concepts of "the ancients" and of that which was "said of old" or "since days of yore" *(pálai légetai)*. Apparently Moltmann regards this appeal to concepts current in antiquity as the unmistakable symptom of a romantic, mythological and archaic view of tradition, a view which ignores or refuses to acknowledge the fundamental distinction between the concept of tradition held in antiquity and the Judaeo-Christian concept. The thing which appears to offend Moltmann most is a thesis which I do in fact advocate and have every intention of continuing to defend in the future: the thesis that a profound analogy exists between what Plato meant by the "ancients" and what Christian theology understands by a "prophet", a "hagiographer", an "inspired" author. I suspect that the objection to this thesis involves something more than a mere misunderstanding which can be cleared up fairly easily. I suspect, in fact, that it may also reflect a basic difference, which is not so easy to eliminate, between the "Protestant" and "Catholic" attitudes toward authority and tradition. But first let us clear up the misunderstanding: I do not believe, any more than Plato did, that "the truth is always intimately bound up with the old", or that the mere fact that something has been said "since time immemorial" represents a "certification of truth". The "wisdom of the ancients" can be certified as "true" only if it was derived from a divine source. Plato too made this fact perfectly clear.

Moltmann goes on to say: "Thus in this view, revelation stands at the beginning of tradition." I would not necessarily regard this assertion as an objection to my thesis, although it was clearly intended as a criticism; for I could in fact accept it as it stands. That is, I do in fact believe that the nucleus of the various mythic traditions of the world (difficult as it may often be to identify this nucleus) represents the echo or reminiscence of a primordial revelation which took place at the beginning of human history. In this sense I consider it justifiable to allude to our primal origins, to the dawn of history, in the way implied by the use of the phrase *pálai légetai*. On the other hand, the analysis of my views which I have just quoted from

Jürgen Moltmann may bear another interpretation which I would *not* be able to accept, and in this case I would really consider it a valid objection to my thesis. It would, in fact, be a valid objection if it implies the rejection of a view of tradition in which revelation is, as it were, *by definition* something which could have taken place only at the beginning of time. Obviously, no Christian can accept such a view. Plato, on the other hand, had every reason to hold this view, as did the countless other thinkers of pre-Christian or non-Christian cultures, to whom in fact no divine word had penetrated beyond that knowledge embodied, and at the same time partially concealed, in the mythological tales handed down "from days of yore": knowledge of how the world was born out of the ungrudging goodness of the Creator, knowledge of the perfection and the fall of the primordial human being, knowledge of the judgment which awaits us on the other side of death, and so on.

One's response to another question posed by Jürgen Moltmann will depend on whether or not one accepts this idea of a primordial revelation and of a "sacred tradition" derived from this revelation. Moltmann's question is: "Are we to equate the Apostles with the Ancients of Plato?" Of course I myself would not use the term "equate", but I would say —and actually did so in my little book on the concept of tradition—that the two "have a great deal in common". A major trait which the Apostles and the Ancients have in common is that both groups represent the original recipients of what Plato calls "knowledge imparted from a divine source above", and moreover, both groups represent the earliest links in the chain of tradition forged as a result of this knowledge. However, they have something else in common which is even more important, namely the origin of the message imparted to them: for the truth of the mythic tradition derives from the same Logos which became incarnate in Christ.

As for Moltmann's next question, as to whether "the content of the Greek tradition which existed 'from days of yore'" is equivalent to the content of the Christian Gospel", I would reply without a moment's hesitation that of course neither Plato nor any other inhabitant of a pre-Christian or non-Christian culture can have had the slightest intimation of the Incarnation of God or of the Passion and Resurrection of Christ. Nevertheless, a man of the stature of Thomas Aquinas did not hesitate to say that even people who had not actually been exposed, in an explicit form, to the revelation of Christ, might be capable of the belief "that God would redeem mankind in a manner pleasing to himself", which in effect involves the concept of implicit faith in Christ, of believing with a *fide implicita*. Thus, once again, I believe that we should give some thought to the possibility that, despite the uniqueness and the radical "novelty" of the revelation of Christ, there might nevertheless be something in common between the "sacred tradition" of which, for example, Plato speaks, and the Christian Gospel—at least in the sense that both traditions tell us that God himself stands warranty for the meaning of the world and for man's salvation.

In any case, I am convinced that it is legitimate, possible and perhaps even necessary to regard the revelation and promise imparted to us in Christ as intimately linked to the primordial origins of human history, as well as to pre-Christian and non-Christian peoples and to what—in an admittedly distorted form in which it has become overgrown and often almost unrecognizable, but never lost—these peoples have "from time immemorial" and "from days of yore" believed to be sacred truth, and preserved down through the millennia. After all, the concept of *pálai légetai*, of what was said by them of old, appears not only in Plato, but also in the New Testament, in the first verse of the Epistle to the Hebrews. Thus—not *before* us but *behind* us—there looms a horizon, a horizon of the past whence all things are derived, which reaches back to the dawn of history, and beyond that to a time when time itself did not exist.

Now that I am nearing the end of this exposition, I will attempt to formulate some kind of conclusion, which will take the shape of questions.

If existence as a rational being implies, in effect, that we live our lives *vis-à-vis de l'univers,* confronting the whole of reality and the totality of that which is, and that we make the response appropriate to the reality which reveals itself in our experience, our thought and our faith—can this existential response be oriented exclusively toward that which is to come, as if God were solely "the absolute future"and not *at the same time* the absolute *origin* of man and all created things? As if he were not the "Ancient of Days" *as well as* he whom St. Augustine describes as "younger than all"? As if God, as a central Now, did not encompass all the dimensions of temporal duration? As if everything we are able to do and plan on our own initiative were not always derived from the gift of creation and our own created nature, which were ordained long ago and which we encounter as something preexistent? As if we did not yet dare to call anything "good", despite the fact that God himself called everything which he had made "very good"? As if, moreover, Christ were only the "Omega Point" and not to the same degree the Alpha; the first *and* the last, the same yesterday, today, and for ever: *qui est et qui erat et qui venturus est* (He "which is and which was and which is to come", Rev 1:8; cf. Rev 22:13)? As if the Incarnation of God had not in fact already taken place, "in the fullness of time" and as if the incarnate Logos were not already really dwelling among us, in the form of his revealed Word and in the sacrament of the Eucharist? As if nothing existed but that which is "still to come"? As if everything were yet to be hoped for, and as if there were nothing to remember and nothing for which to give thanks?

I realize that in the last paragraph I formulated the views of the "Opposition" in somewhat extreme terms and that probably no one is likely to identify with these views as I have expressed them. Nevertheless, I do not regard it as an idle exercise to carry out to their logical, indeed their most radical, conclusions, certain approaches or tendencies which actually exist among contemporary theologians, both Protestant and Catholic. For this exercise might well reveal the image of a theological anthropology which keeps silent regarding what man *is* "by nature," i.e., by virtue of his created state, or which may even go so far as to declare the entire question of human nature devoid of interest. Moreover, it might reveal a theology whose proponents no longer regard it as their primary task to preserve the identity and maintain the presence in our consciousness, over the passage of time, of God's revelation to man, but who instead are concerned with reflecting and interpreting in "up-to-date" or "relevant" terms the religious, or purely "utopian", i.e., sociopolitical, impulses of their time, at times through the use of biblical concepts and terminology.

It is logical and, so to speak, proper that in a theology such as this, the category of "the future" would assume a unique significance and might even become the exclusive focus of concern. Of course, one wonders whether the liberation from our nature and our past which Roger Garaudy views as the aim of the new theology and praises in such glowing terms would not inevitably lead to that disastrous type of freedom which, because it is "pilfered" by forgetting the past, necessarily ends up being empty. In fact, would it not lead to that famous "essenceless" freedom of which the Existentialists speak and which necessitates our starting over "from scratch" because to accept anything preexistent would *eo ipso* amount to receiving something [a sort of essence] from the past? I have another question: Will not the hope which, once again quite logically, will in all likelihood constitute virtually the sole concern of this new theology inevitably turn out to be—to put it mildly—a rather problematical affair? For after all, hope does not simply involve the expectation that something good will happen to us in the future; it also involves *hav-*

ing grounds for such expectation! But the grounds for hope, insofar as such grounds in fact exist, do *not*, like that which is hoped for, lie in the future. Instead these grounds *must already exist* or even have existed for a long time, and thus are prior to, and a precondition of, all possible hope. It is logically impossible for me to hope that a reason may exist for me to hope. But there is no other way for me to find out this reason than to *remember* it in the course of reflection and contemplation.

The future is void without a past. And a hope without foundation—without a foundation which preexists our hope as well as ourselves—might just as well be called despair.

58

The Art of Not Yielding to Despair

If one accepts or even is willing to seriously ponder that concept of the temporal end of human history which has been an active feature of Western historical thought from the days of John on Patmos down to the time of Vladimir Soloviev, who in the final year of the nineteenth century published his myth of the Antichrist—i.e., the notion that the end of history (we should bear in mind that we are speaking of history *within* the framework of time!) will be characterized not by the triumph of "reason" or justice or Christianity, but rather by something in the nature of a universal catastrophe for which one of the most appropriate names is "the reign of the Antichrist", a

Problems of Modern Faith, pp. 175–90, translated by Jan van Heurck. © 1985 Franciscan Herald Press, Chicago. Reprinted with permission.

term implying the worldwide dominion of evil, a pseudo-order maintained by violence, and so on—if, I say, one regards this conception of history as something which at least merits serious thought, then of course one is immediately confronted by certain questions, and by two questions in particular. *First,* does this conception of a catastrophic end to history within time possess any degree of internal probability, given our empirical knowledge of the historical process and of historical trends? In other words, do things "look as if" they might turn out this way? If one's answer to this question is "yes," then the *second* question is: What is to become of man's hopes for the future, and is not the only appropriate response to human history one of despair?

Let us first address the question of what internal evidence exists for the probability or improbability of a catastrophic end to history. Unquestionably there have been eras in which the notion that history might conceivably have an "unhappy end" may have, or even must have, seemed completely incomprehensible. On the other hand, today our inventory of empirical data regarding current historical trends at least suggests that certain phenomena which await us in the future may not in fact be far removed from those foretold by apocalyptic vision. Thus, to state the matter in negative terms, it does *not* look as if Immanuel Kant will be right in his prediction that the unfolding of the historical process itself will result in the foundation of the Kingdom of God on earth; nor does it even appear that this process will lead to the creation of a middle-class society capable of administering universal justice. Moreover, from the purely empirical standpoint there is very little evidence to suggest that the mere act of altering the system of production and making changes in the relative distribution of wealth is capable of alleviating human injustice or limiting the abuse of power, much less of eliminating them altogether. Of course, I do not for a moment mean to suggest that we should abandon our struggle to create a just social order, by means of the more equable distribution of wealth as well as by other means. Nor do I dispute the fact that, generally speaking, we have made steady progress in the sphere of achieving social justice and that this progress is still going forward. However, I do consider improbable the idea that such social amelioration could ever bring about world conditions in which, as Ernst Bloch has expressed it, man would cease to be a wolf to other men and instead would treat him in a manner befitting a human being. We simply cannot anticipate that the "transformation of the world through socialism" is really capable of creating Bloch's "world without disillusion". Not only have more than fifty years of the implementation of Marxist policies failed to provide any empirical evidence in support of this thesis, but the thesis itself is intrinsically highly improbable because, as Franz Borkenau states, the moral justification of a lawless dictatorship and the expectation of the total disappearance of every form of asocial egoism are mutually contradictory ideas. Today orthodox Marxists no longer like to speak of those rosy expectations which characterized their movement at the outset, but nevertheless these expectations continue to fire the dynamics of Marxist revolution. We all know that Ernst Bloch was accused of deviation from the party line because of his book *Das Prinzip Hoffnung* ["The Principle of Hope"]. But it should not be forgotten that Karl Marx himself called Communism "the true resolution of man's conflict with nature and with man" and "the solution of the riddle of history"; and that in the year of the Russian Revolution (1917), Lenin, speaking of "the Communist society", stated that in this society, for the first time, human beings would "obey the basic rules governing social life . . . which have been known from time immemorial" and would do so "without violence, without coercion". But as I have stated, there is little evidence that these predictions will be fulfilled. In his book *Gespräche mit Stalin* ["Conversations with Stalin"], the leading Yugoslavian Communist Milovan Djilas discusses the belief which developed, during the battles of World War II, among "Soviet officers who had been raised on Marxist doctrine" and which an army commander reported to Djilas: the belief that the triumph of Marxism throughout the world would result in wars of unprecedented savagery, and only then would the ruthless extermination of human beings reach its peak, "for the sake of the greater good"!

Naturally there is such a thing as historical "progress". Advances in medicine, agricultural technology and the science of breeding livestock are the only things which have made it physically possible for millions of people to survive on this earth. Most remarkable of all are the great advances which have been made in the sphere of the technological domination of nature and the exploitation of its resources. Of course in this area there are a "but" and a "nevertheless" to consider. Technological advances have always possessed the character of *opportunities*; and as we all know, it is possible to take advantage of an opportunity; but it is also possible to "let it slip" or to waste it. I will cite only two examples of the ambivalence of technological progress, both of which relate to the theme of this discussion. The first example is that of research into the psychosomatic or psychophysical reality of man. Never before has investigation in this field revealed as many new techniques for healing man's ills as it is doing today. However, it is equally true that these same techniques have created unprecedented potentialities for man to seduce, enslave and forcibly modify the nature of other men. A second example is that of atomic energy. At this point no one can predict whether the dangers of physical destruction and political abuse inherent in man's control of atomic energy will eventually be outweighed by the potential of putting it to some meaningful use.

We have asked whether there exist any clues or signs which indicate the possibility, or even the probability, of a catastrophic end to history within time. In attempting to answer this question I would like, for the time being, to refrain from expressing my own views, and instead present for our consideration statements drawn from other contemporary writers. (Naturally this approach does not imply that I accept without reservation the validity of every opinion I cite; I simply maintain that, in view of what is going on in the world today, it is conceivable for people to think and to say such things.) For example, Johan Huizinga states: "It would be instructive if one could see represented by a curve on a graph the rapidity with which the word 'progress' has disappeared from the vocabulary of nations all over the world." In a letter written in 1942, Thomas Mann declares that the experiences of the past few years have made him lose faith "in the pure and unsubdued will of the world to resist evil"; one could, he says, perhaps call this attitude a symptom of emigrants' psychosis "and even lack of faith", but nevertheless there is a "difference between believing in goodness and believing in the triumph of goodness on earth". Hermann Rauschning, formerly president of the Senate of the Free City of Danzig, who later settled in the United States, states that in modern nihilism "an essential trait of man has entered fully into historical consciousness: his yearning for self-destruction". At the London Symposium on Man and His Future, a scientific conference held in 1962 which has since given rise to much debate, the participants discussed, among other things, the disturbing question of whether we may not have reached the stage at which it is no longer possible for man to maintain control over those factors on which his future fate depends. At the same time they voiced their suspicion that it might well make no difference to the outcome if policy decisions were left up to scientists rather than to politicians. Their conclusions could be summarized in the statement, attributed to Robert Oppenheimer, that the possibility of apocalypse has become a reality of our lives.

It seems difficult to imagine a human being who lived in the eighteenth or nineteenth century saying things similar to the remarks I have just quoted. (Of course in actual fact some people *did* say things of this sort then, for Christians have never abandoned apocalyptic prophecy. But in those days no one really took them seriously.) But what is it that has happened between then and now? One possible reply is that now we live with the threat of the hydrogen bomb. This is quite true, but has the nature of man in history really changed?

At this point one might interject the remark that the idea of the "catastrophic end" of history is still a far cry from the notion of the "reign of the Antichrist" and of the universal totalitarian regime of evil! Or have these notions too by this time acquired a certain degree of internal probability? In his effort to avoid the "excesses" of the "medieval" conceptions of the Antichrist by adopting a strictly rationalistic and "progressive" attitude, the noted theologian and historian Ignaz von Döllinger expounded the following "modern" argument in the year 1860: Given the "broadening of our mental horizons with regard to the geographical extent of the earth", the idea of a world power strong enough to organize a universal persecution on all the continents and even "on all the islands", and at the same time to suppress all religious worship, and so on, is "simply inconceivable". Reading such an argument today, we can only smile. If there is anything in the world which has a good chance of functioning smoothly, it is the technical apparatus for the maintenance of dictatorial power; "islands" no longer exist. Obviously the vision of Döllinger's contemporary Friedrich Nietzsche was far more penetrating, although of course Nietzsche was less concerned with technological potentials than he was with man himself: despite all the talk of "civilization" and "progress", "the democratization of Europe", Nietzsche claimed, would end "in the creation of a type of man who is, in the most subtle sense, trained for *slavery*", and at the same time represented "an involuntary arrangement for the breeding of *tyrants* in every sense of the word". If one follows the trail of this terrifying thought down through history, one is surprised to find how frequently it has been expressed since Nietzsche's time. For example, Albert Camus says that, although freedom exists at the beginning of every revolution, eventually the time will come when justice demands the elimination of freedom, and the revolution ends in a reign of terror. Ernst Jünger states that the present-day expansion of extraterritorial spheres of influence, which is leading toward the establishment of a global order, i.e., a *single* universal state, "brings with it the fear that the attempt to perfect the system at the expense of freedom [may assume] the most radical forms". The sociologist Wilhelm Röpke expresses his fear that, once they have grown accustomed to the high degree of control their government exercises over their lives, people "may no longer attach much importance to the residuum of freedom which lies between them and absolute government control". Hermann Rauschning believes that the world is evolving "toward the establishment of an absolute center of power, a universal absolutism", and he speaks of the danger that we may develop an international civilization characterized by "a materialistic hedonism based on progressive dehumanization [and] ruled by a universal Grand Inquisitor who holds a total monopoly on power". As we all know, the concept of the "Grand Inquisitor" derives from the myth which Dostoevsky incorporated into his great novel *The Brothers Karamazov,* where we find the disconcerting sentence: "In the end they will lay down their freedom at our feet and say: 'Make us your slaves, if only you will feed us!' " Furthermore, this same sentence is quoted in one of the most remarkable and thought-provoking books of recent times, Aldous Huxley's *Brave New World Revisited.* In 1931 Huxley had published the highly intelligent science-fiction novel *Brave New World,* whose title was drawn from Shakespeare's *The Tempest,* and whose events take place in the sixth and seventh centuries "after Ford" (A.F.). Thirty years later the author reexamines this book: "In 1931, when *Brave New World* was being written, I was convinced that there was still plenty of time. The completely organized society . . . the abolition of free will by methodical conditioning, the servitude made acceptable . . . —these things were coming all right, but not in my time, not even in the time of my grandchildren . . . In this third quarter of the twentieth century . . . I feel a good deal less optimistic . . . The prophecies made in 1931 are coming true much sooner than I thought." Then Huxley reviews his earlier book point by point and, on the basis of his experience of historical events which took place during the intervening years, predicts a future in which one of the most important elements will be a "scientific dictatorship" in which "there will probably be much less violence than under Hitler and Stalin", and in which individuals "will be painlessly regimented by a corps of highly trained social engineers". To be sure, "democracy and freedom will be the theme of every broadcast and editorial", but "the underlying substance will be a new kind of non-violent totalitarianism", which it will be virtually impossible to overthrow. It would appear that Gabriel Marcel's surmise that the concentration camps may reveal "the image of the world to come" is already obsolete. "Non-violent totalitarianism" is the most inhuman form of totalitarianism—among other reasons because it can always cite what appear to be valid arguments to prove that it is not what in fact it is. This consummate mendacity must inevitably result in the atrophy of communication between human beings, which is essentially based on trust. Martin Buber attempted to express this fact in the following terms: "In the future we may expect the total reciprocity of existential distrust to develop to a point at which speech will revert to silence." (Of course not only does this breakdown in communication fail to eliminate "idle chatter" and mere verbiage [verbositas], but it actually encourages them.) The possibility of such a breakdown in communication, Huxley says, never for a moment occurred to the early advocates of universal literacy and the freedom of the press: "They did not foresee what in fact has happened . . . the development of a vast mass communications industry, concerned . . . neither with the true nor the false, but with the unreal, the more or less totally irrelevant."

Of course not one of the authors I have just quoted speaks so much as a syllable about the "Antichrist". Probably most of them would decline to acknowledge any connection between this term and the ideas they intended to expound. Nevertheless I believe that it would be difficult to deny that the state of affairs adumbrated by all the statements I have quoted corresponds quite closely to what is actually implied by the conception of the "reign of the Antichrist". This correspondence consists above all in the fact that all the authors cited make it clear that it will be *we ourselves* who bring about the end of history, that the catastrophe will not be visited upon us from outside, but will arise out of the historical process itself. Neither the "great engineers" of evolution conjured up by Konrad Lorenz, nor any other *deus ex machina,* nor even God himself, will intervene to save us from ourselves.

Tradidit mundum disputationi eorum (Eccles 3:11); God has turned the world over to men to do with as they see fit. This is the terrible dowry of freedom, which necessarily involves the possibility of abuse. "Everything clearly indicates", says Gabriel Marcel, "that we ourselves have been given the authority to build the walls of the prison in which we want to live. This is the terrible price we pay for the unfathomable power which has been entrusted to us and which, moreover, is the foundation of our selfhood."

At this point we are in a position to experience the full impact of the second question we posed at the beginning of this discussion: What reason do human beings have for *hope* if we must expect temporal history to end in catastrophe? Would not the acceptance of such a view necessarily paralyze, and deprive of value, all active engagement in the historical process? How, under such conditions, can we expect a young person to "set to work with a will"? I will attempt to answer this question in several successive stages.

Point One. We must draw a clear distinction (which people rarely do; I am thinking above all of Ernst Bloch) *on the one hand* between what we regard as desirable, what we can plan for and actually expect to bring about, between the setting of goals and the desire to effect change and *on the other hand,* that which can, in the strict sense of the term, be defined as an object of hope. We must learn this distinction from the inherent wisdom of language itself, which tells us that hope is always directed toward something which we *cannot* achieve ourselves. Thus when we are talking about something which we can bring about ourselves—as can easily be proved through the analysis of colloquial speech—we are not in fact talking about hope. Furthermore—and this is the most important fact to bear in mind—human hope (not *hopes,* but hope, which is always singular) is directed toward an ultimate and perfect satiation of desire. What we truly hope for is, as Ernst Bloch quite accurately states: fullness of life; the restoration or healing of man; a homeland, "coming home", a kingdom; "Jerusalem"; the absolute satisfaction of all our needs; beatitude of a kind we have never known before.

If we accept this definition of hope, we are at once confronted by two questions. *First,* is there any such thing as a goal which we can achieve through the realistic and legitimate will to change the world (the goal of social justice, a classless society, peace among nations, races and religions, and so forth)—is there any goal of this kind from which one can seriously expect or hope to obtain that ultimate fulfillment, that "perfection of existence", of which we have just spoken? The *second* question we must ask ourselves is this: Does anyone really believe that he has the right to regard all engagement in the historical process as meaningless, or to deny its value, simply because it will not ultimately create a world without suffering and injustice, a heaven on earth? This question closely parallels the question of whether we can reasonably maintain that everything we do in this corporeal existence is deprived of value by the fact that in the end we all must die.

Point Two. As far as death is concerned, one thing is clearly apparent: if our historical existence in this world is totally defined by hope and possesses the inherent structure of the "Not-yet" (in this purely phenomenological characterization of human life in terms of hope) Pascal and Ernst Bloch and Gabriel Marcel are in complete agreement with traditional Western anthropology; if, until the very moment of his death, man is really a *viator* or traveler "on his way" to something; and if, even in the final instant of his life, the essential thing, fulfillment, still lies before him—then *either* this hope, which is identical to existence itself, is simply absurd, *or* the satisfaction of this hope lies on the other side of death! Thus anyone who deliberately restricts his field of vision to the domain which lies on this side of the boundary of death, quite understandably sees nothing but futility and absurdity. C. S. Lewis says that the truly unfortunate man is the high-minded unbeliever who is desperately trying not to lose what he calls his faith in man. On the other hand, the ability *not* to yield to despair when confronted with the fact of death, as well as with the prospect of the catastrophic end of temporal history, is a matter of great practical concern to us all. Even in the midst of catastrophe, a person who possesses this ability remains capable of affirmation, which in turn makes it possible for him to engage in activity on the historical plane: to engage, in other words, in "political" activity—activity directed toward the realization of justice—as well as *artistic* activity, whose purpose it is to praise the creation. As Erik Peterson has stated, the mouth of the martyr does not utter a word against God's Creation. Despite everything which befalls him and despite how the world of man must "really" look to him, he still persists in saying: The Creation is good, very good!

Point Three. Viewed in the context I have outlined, the emphatic conviction of Christians that hope represents a "theological" virtue may appear, if not plausible, at least somewhat more plausible than it did before. Apparently Immanuel Kant had something like this theological aspect of hope in mind when he said that the fundamental philosophical (!) question,

"What may I hope for?" is answered *not* by philosophy but by religion. Naturally there are perfectly legitimate hopes which lie, so to speak, "on the hither side" of religion—hopes, let us say, for the welfare of the younger generation or for peace in the world. But can one claim that a person who abandons one of these hopes (hopes in the *plural!*) and is unable to maintain it any longer is actually "in the wrong"? For a human being, being right, being "in order", is precisely what is meant by "virtue". Thus hope constitutes an element of human "rightness" not merely by virtue of the fact that it is hope, but because it aims at *true* fulfillment, which, if it happens at all, will take place "beyond" our corporeal and historical existence, and of which we "know" only through faith.

Point Four. The object of the theological, "supernatural" hope of the Christian must not be conceived as something wholly divorced from human existence in this world. To be sure, it lies "beyond" the boundary of death, which, both in the personal history of the individual and in the universal history of mankind separates man from his own perfection. Nevertheless, on the practical level, this object of supernatural hope is closely bound up with those images of hope which play a role in the life of the natural man; moreover, it also affects his actual conduct within the sphere of history. When apocalyptic prophecy speaks of the resurrection of the body and of the "New Earth", it is in fact telling us that not one iota, not one jot or tittle of everything in this life which was good and right, just, true, beautiful, fine and salutary will ever be lost. "The world will [be] harvested and the harvest brought home", Hans Urs von Balthasar says in his interpretation of Soloviev; but of course he adds that it will not be brought home "by mankind itself".

One of the great recurrent symbols and images of hope by which men have, from the dawn of history, sought to represent the ultimate fulfillment of human existence is that of the Great Banquet. In the *Phaedrus* Plato spoke of this banquet as something which takes place beyond time and above the heavens. But the communal meal in which Christians, while still in the world of history, apprehend and, in a real sense, celebrate the beginning and the foretaste of their life of beatitude at the table of God—this kind of fellowship, this kind of banquet is something which Plato never dreamed of. For even the dream that such a thing is possible remains inaccessible to all those forced to rely on the unaided reason.

Nevertheless there is some reason to believe that whenever human beings endow with the power of their hope the image of a perfect society of the future, a society in which man will no longer be the wolf of man but his brother, and in which the goods of life are distributed justly, this image may secretly refer to that Great Banquet—regardless of whether the object of hope is labeled "democracy", "the reign of freedom", "the classless society", or any other of a hundred names. In any case, the fact that such utopian expectations regarding the future are frequently converted into "religious" absolutes reveals that—contrary though this notion may be to the programmatic views of their proponents—their ultimate aim is the attainment of something which cannot possibly be attained through any effort to reform the world through socialism or any other political or economic program. In such cases, one suspects, there in fact exists a subterranean link between "secular" and Christian hope—always assuming of course that those who place their hope in a future society are really aiming toward the creation of a *universal* human community and that their program does not at the same time involve their personal acquisition of dictatorial powers, the practice of discrimination, or the intention to liquidate any "others" who do not belong to their "in-group".

Granted this condition, one could—by way of analogy to the concept of *fides implicita* or implicit faith, by virtue of which, as the great Western theologians have always maintained, anyone who believes God capable of redeeming man in any way pleasing to himself may "by implication" or "in effect" be considered to believe in Christ—one could, I say, logically speak of a *spes implicita* as well, an implicit *hope* by virtue of which a person implicitly (not expressly) hopes for the same thing the Christian hopes for. Of course the mutuality of their hope can be perceived only from the standpoint of *explicit* hope. In other words, if Christians do not perceive such common factors and recognize them for what they are, then no one will do so; and in this case they will have no power to shape history. Of course, the mere fact that two groups "have something in common" does not make them identical, and what Romano Guardini calls the task of "distinguishing that which is Christian" from that which is not is a never-ending one, of particularly pressing importance at the present time.

Two elements are involved in this task. The first is the need to confirm and maintain awareness of the crucial insight that, precisely because of the irrevocable "Not-yet" structure of historical existence, the ultimate fulfillment of human hope (*not* hopes) cannot be realized this side of death. Second, it must be made clear that (and why) the object of this hope, which is at bottom identical with our existence itself, is by its very nature something which cannot be exhaustively described or "nailed down", and cannot be formulated in terms of clearly defined plans and goals, or eschatological schemata. Instead, the man who truly hopes, like the man who prays, must remain open to a fulfillment of which he knows neither in what hour nor in what form it will finally come.

Naturally the art of not yielding to despair is not something which one can simply *learn*. Like all other "arts", and indeed to a far greater degree than any other, it is a gift. Nevertheless, it is possible to specify certain conditions which, whether by means of conscious reflection or not, must first be fulfilled, if we are to prove capable of receiving this gift.

59

"Eternal Life"

The full force of this idea of happiness as action emerges still more clearly when we see that it is linked in a cohesive logical structure with several of the basic tenets of Western teachings on man and reality in general. These are, above all, the following three propositions. First: *Happiness means perfection.* Essential to the concept of happiness is that there is "nothing left to wish for", that the happy person has attained the ultimate goal. "In perfect felicity the whole man is perfected." Second: *Perfection means full realization.* Man attains perfection insofar as the incomplete draft which he is initially is realized attains to fullest reality. If happiness is equivalent to perfection, then "Felicity must consist in man's attainment of the uttermost degree of being real". Third: *Realization is achieved by action.* This does not mean here that only fussing and straining will yield results. The meaning is rather: "Action is the ultimate realization of the person who acts." That is to say, only by acting does man achieve the fullness of his reality. Naturally, he is already real in the sense that he exists before he acts; without existence he could not very well act. That is taken for granted. But there is a mode of achieving reality which goes beyond the mere fact of existing, in which living beings attain to a more intense and "realer" realness — by acting. Happiness, then, as drinking of the drink, must be thought of as a form

Happiness and Contemplation, pp. 53–55, translated by Richard and Clara Winston. © 1958 Pantheon Books, Inc., New York. Used with permission.

of acting which opens all the potentialities of man to fullest realization.

This, says Thomas, is also the meaning of the phrase dear to the Scriptures when referring to beatitude: Eternal Life. The term does not mean simply living without end, but the supreme intensification of the state of being alive in a perfect "living–doing" (whereas the conversion of action to its opposite signifies a diminution of life, and is therefore aptly called *passio* in both senses, that of passivity and that of suffering, whose final and ultimate form is death).

Index